CRIME SHEFFIELD

from deer poachers to gangsters, 1300 to the 1980s

J. P. BEAN
D. & D. Publications

Front cover: artist's impression of the execution of Charlie Peace, from the Illustrated Police News of March 1879.

First Published by
Sheffield City Libraries in 1987.

New edition 1993
by D & D Publications
PO Box 225
Sheffield S11 7DD
England

ISBN 0-9507645-1-5

CONTENTS

AUTHOR'S NOTE

This book is written for the general reader and is intended as an insight into crime, policing and punishment in Sheffield from feudal times. Records prior to the 18th Century are scarce, presenting difficulties in adopting a uniform approach to the overall period covered by the book. However, there is, I hope, sufficient detail in the early chapters to give a significant impression of the times when beggars were branded, petty thieves hanged, and the parish constable was armed with a musket. From the early 19th Century onwards I have concentrated on those incidents and episodes which made the greatest impact in their day, while noting trends and developments up until the present decade.

For their assistance in the research for this book I am very grateful to: staff of the Local History and Archives Sections of Sheffield City Libraries; South Yorkshire County Record Office; Sheffield Newspapers Ltd.; the Chief Constable, South Yorkshire Police; Alex Hawkins, ex-Detective Inspector, Sheffield City Police; and Tony Fry, former Assistant Editor, *Morning Telegraph*.

J. P. Bean 1987

LORD, LEET AND CONSTABLE

Law and order in medieval England was the preserve of the landed nobility. The lord of the manor administered justice. He alone had the power to mete out capital punishment, to order malefactors to be whipped or tortured, and, in his manorial courts, to collect fines from petty offenders.

In the barony of Hallamshire, an area comprising the parishes of Sheffield, Ecclesall and Bradfield, successive lords from the Norman Conquest onwards exercised these powers. After Magna Carta in 1215 manorial courts were forbidden to deal with felonies – serious offences such as homicide, rape, arson, larceny and burglary – and such cases from Sheffield were heard at York Assizes or West Riding Quarter Sessions. However, punishment of the guilty remained a local matter and records indicate that in 1428 one John Kay was hanged in Sheffield for horse stealing, and in 1495 John Dore suffered a similar fate for murder. Unfortunately no more details of these early victims of the hangman's noose, or of their crimes, are known.

The manorial court combined criminal and civil cases. In 1297 Thomas, Lord Furnival, in his famous charter to the free tenants of Sheffield, included a clause whereby his bailiffs would hold a court every three weeks, with offenders being tried and fined by their peers. The court, known as the Court Leet or Sembly Quest, was held initially at Sheffield Castle and later on Sembly Green, now known as the Wicker. This Court Leet dealt with all minor criminal cases, known as trespasses, together with matters pertaining to weights and measures, the scouring of ditches, cutting of hedges and the "ryngyng of swyne". Under a statute of Edward II in 1325, Court Leets were instructed to inquire into those people "as continually haunt taverns, as sleep by day and watch by night, and eat and drink well, and have nothing."

In addition to the three-weekly Sheffield Court Leets, a Great Tourn of Hallamshire was held twice-yearly. The tourn was a court of Saxon origin, in most areas presided over by the sheriff of the county, but in Hallamshire it was held by the lord of the manor. This was a result of a declaration made by Thomas, Lord Furnival, during the reign of Edward I, that his own bailiffs would perform all duties normally undertaken by the king's bailiffs in Hallamshire. Subsequent lords refused to allow the sheriff, the representative of royal authority within the county, to enter Hallamshire.

Fortunately there are surviving records of Sheffield Court Leet and the Tourn of Hallamshire. Written on sheepskins sewn end to end – the first court roll, beginning 1371, takes up sixteen skins and is twenty-six feet in length – and transcribed by T. Walter Hall earlier this century, they reveal a fascinating insight into local crime in the Middle Ages.

Violence was a regular occurrence – not surprising in an age when men carried knives or swords as a matter of course, and an inclination towards fighting was considered an admirable quality. On 18th April, 1441, John Lastles, who "drew the blood" of John Whete, was fined 6/8d. Richard Falke was fined the same amount for a similar offence on William, son of John Shemyld, of Little Sheffield. Provocation appears to have been considered as seriously as a resultant assault, with Robert Fulford, whose blood had been "drawn" by Robert Swyft, fined 3/4d – the same as his assailant – because he had "given occasion therefor". Public unruliness seems to have been prevalent, too, with many cases of affray dealt with by fines of up to ten shillings.

Numerous cases concerned offences against property, especially the lord's property. In 1440, John Barker the Younger was fined 2d for fishing the lord's waters without permission, while John Shoter had to pay 8d for causing annoyance to the lord by occupying his land. There were fines for taking green wood from Rivelin, damaging saplings at Burngreave, and for felling the lord's oaks at Walkley Bank.

Petty thefts were commonplace, with both men and women fined for stealing items ranging from a stockfish out of a private milldam to a pair of shoes at Sheffield Fair. More serious thefts, like those alleged at the Great Tourn of Easter 1441 to have been committed by Thomas Reyner, were passed on to the superior court. Reyner, it was said, stole a hive of bees at Wadsley and "stealthily took six yards of linen worth threepence a yard" at Waldorshelf. His case was all the more interesting because at the same court a man named Robert Lymehurst was destrained 2/- for going to the house of Thomas Reyner by night and being found secretly hidden their with the latter's wife.

The tourn of April 1565 gives an indication of the legal constraints placed on individual freedom at the time. A fine of 3/4d was imposed on Thomas Pereson for having four men in his house at unlawful hours of the night. The men were fined 1/- each. Unlawful hours were between nine pm, when the curfew bell rang for people to go to bed, and six am when they had to get up for work. The intention behind this legislation was to prevent the hatching of conspiracies and plots.

Strict laws also applied to the playing of games. In the 15th Century there were many cases where fines were imposed on people for playing dice at night, and by a later statute of Henry VIII certain other games, for example bowls, cards and tennis, became unlawful. Anyone who kept premises where such games were played was liable to a fine of £2 per day, and a person caught playing there faced 6/8d for each offence. The object of this act was to prevent people wasting their time and the bailiffs and constables of the manor made monthly searches for gaming houses. One offender, fined 20/- in 1564 for "playing at unlawful games within his house", was Richard Shay, deputy bailiff of Bradfield.

Some curious cases make up the remainder of the Manorial Court records. There is a fine of 12d for a man who "was not willing to give five quarters for one yard in his art of a weaver." Three men were fined 3/4d each for insulting the Vicar of Glossop. A fine of the same amount was imposed on William Sylvester "for that he hath not kept his maister's dogge moosselled", and 6/8d on Thomas Swallow the Younger for keeping a greyhound. In 1578 a long list of miscreants were fined for wearing hats instead of caps in Sheffield Church. This was contrary to a statute of 1570 designed to benefit the ailing English cap manufacturing trade.

Rape was a felony with which the local courts could not deal. There is only one case of rape in the available records for Sheffield Manorial Court, that of William Alene who, it was alleged in 1564, "at the feast of the invention of the Holy Cross came to the house of Joan Hevylegh by night and there made an assault upon her with the intention of rape, to her hurt." Cases of rape were rare in the Middle Ages and ones such as this would be heard at the Quarter Sessions.

By granting his people a regular court, Lord Furnival was not simply dispensing goodwill or encouraging democracy. His ancestors' methods of exacting tolls had been unpopular and Furnival clearly saw an advantage in collecting revenue in the form of fines, rather than the old ways of feudal service or extortion.

As to how the fines were paid there is no local record, but considerable hardship must have been experienced on many occasions. In 1552 a labourer earned twenty-six shillings per year; a chief hind, carter or shepherd twenty shillings; a common husbandry servant sixteen shillings; and a female servant ten shillings. The income of most defendants in Sheffield Manorial Court would have been within this range and clearly fines of 3/4d for wearing a hat instead of a cap, 10/- for cutting down a tree, and 20/- for playing at unlawful games must have been financially crippling.

In addition to fining petty offenders and committing felons to the quarter sessions and assizes, the manorial court appointed parish constables. The township of Sheffield, with a population calculated at 2207 in 1615, had two constables, while the neighbouring townships of Bradfield, Handsworth and Ecclesfield each had one.

The duties of the constable were arduous. He was appointed to ensure that the peace was kept, to arrest wrongdoers, eavesdroppers, nightwalkers and vagrants and to lock them up. He collected fines and taxes and, in many parishes, inflicted such punishments as the flogging of criminals and the branding of vagrants.

Vagrancy and the relief of the poor, aged and infirm was an acute social problem in the later Middle Ages. Following the Black Death, which swept the country in 1348-9 and reduced the population by half, extensive labour legislation was introduced. The Statute of Labourers in 1351 decreed that all villages should have stocks, to be used as an open gaol for runaway servants and labourers. An act of 1388 prohibited labourers from departing their place of residence without a certificate from a justice of the peace. In 1531 Henry VIII directed the justices to assign to the "impotent poor" a limited area in which they could beg, while beggars considered to be "sturdy" were to be whipped. Shortly afterwards, compulsory charity was introduced, the deserving poor to be assisted while the penalties for vagrancy were made more severe. Thus a "sturdy beggar" was whipped for a first offence, his right ear cut off for a second, and if he offended again he was put to death.

This act was considered to be a little excessive and in 1547 Edward VI substituted slavery for the death penalty. A person who would not work was to be branded with the letter V and adjudged a slave for two years, to any person who wanted him. He was to be fed only on bread and water and made to work by beating, chaining, or whatever means his master saw fit. If he ran away during the two years he was to be branded with the letter S on his cheek and adjudged a slave for life. If he ran away again he was sentenced to death.

This latter act also made provision for the "impotent poor". They were to be conveyed by the officers of each parish on horseback, cart or foot to the constable of the next parish, and so on from constable to constable until they eventually arrived at either the place they were born, or had lived for at least three years. There they were to be maintained by parish funds and in 1572 Elizabeth I introduced a tax specifically for this purpose, to be collected by the justices.

The local implications of all this legislation can be seen from the records of fees paid to the town constables by the Church Burgesses and Town Trustees. In 1580 there are entries of 8d for carrying a lame man to the next constable; 2/- for carrying "certain rogues" to Rotherham; and items for carrying "pykers" – tramps or vagabonds – to Barnsley, and a beggar to Worksop. The following year 6d was given by the constable to "a poore blind man" who had the Queen's letters patent – written authorization to beg in a certain district.

In 1592 the constables conveyed a maid out of town "that came from London in time of plag." Other items relate to carrying cripples and poor wenches, assisting lame soldiers, and carrying a boy in a barrow to the next constable. In 1594 1/- was paid to Constable Yowle for carrying a lunatic named Hepwood out of town. Unfortunates such as this man were sometimes kept chained up, but more often taken to the parish boundary and set at large. Hepwood was perhaps luckier than most, if only in that he was given 6d to help him on his way.

Gypsies, who had arrived in England around the turn of the 16th Century, were regarded in the same light as robbers and felons. Henry VIII legislated heavily against them and they were made very unwelcome in the towns. In 1595 a payment was made to the town watchmen for their work "when the Gypsees were in the towne."

The parish constable held his post for one year, each man of the parish supposedly taking a turn. In a parish the size of Sheffield, however, it is likely that appointments were made on the basis of suitability as, unlike the smaller, more isolated parishes, there would be men willing to occupy the post.

There was no salary, fees paid were dependant upon duties undertaken, and at times the work must have been dangerous. In 1613 a sum of 2/- was provided for the Sheffield constables to purchase "a new bandilerowe". This was a broadbelt, worn over the shoulders, which helped to support a musket and had twelve small cases attached, each containing a musket charge.

Besides maintaining the vagrancy laws, the constable spent much of his time escorting felons to the justice of the peace, and also to York Castle. He carried out warrants of search and arrest, issued by the justice, and was responsible for leading the hue and cry – the traditional pursuit which occurred following the commission of a felony. His responsibility for the night watch – the period between curfew bell and day bell – was largely delegated to the town waits, men who combined the duty of watchman with that of town piper, entertaining at town functions when not on watch.

Another aspect of the constable's work involved the punishment of offenders. It was his responsibility to place miscreants in the stocks, pillory, cucking stool and scold's bridle. Both men and women were publicly whipped on occasion but there is no clear evidence of this taking place locally before the mid 18th Century.

The first mention of stocks in Sheffield is in 1576, although it is probable that they had been in existence since the Statute of Labourers over two centuries earlier. The stocks were situated at the present junction of Church Street and High Street, beside the Church Gates, facing down High Street. They were moved to Paradise Square around the turn of the 19th Century, remaining in use there for another thirty years. There were other stocks in the area at Bridgehouses, Attercliffe and on Sheffield Moor.

Like most towns, Sheffield had a town cage – an early version of a police cell where the constable could lock up felons until he had time to take them to the justice of the peace to be examined. Among items relating to the cage is a sum paid for maintenance in 1613, and another, of £7/1/2d in 1652 for building a new one. The town cage no doubt went out of service when Sheffield's first Town Hall, with cells beneath it, was opened in 1700.

The pillory, erected by the Town Trustees in 1571, stood in Castle Foulds, the area of Exchange Street which lies alongside Castle Market. Pillories were originally introduced to bring public shame on cheats, especially those who had given short measure or weight, but all types of petty offender found their way into them.

Parishes who did not keep a cucking stool were liable to prosecution. The cucking stool was a seat in which cheats and brawlers, as well as nagging women, were chained and locked either in a public place where they were jeered at and pelted, or by pond or river into which they were periodically ducked. In 1580 the Town Trustees provided for the making of a "cuck stoole". New ones followed in 1616 and 1636, and in 1654 6/2d was paid to the constables for "rynging the bells on 5th November, mending the stocks and bringing the cucke stool up to Barker Poole." The last reference to the stool is in 1747 when 1/- was paid for retrieving it from the river.

As the Middle Ages passed, the administration of justice, once the exclusive right of the lord, became less a privilege and more a responsibility. While retaining overall jurisdiction over his Manorial Court, and benefiting financially from it, Lord Furnival at least sowed the seeds of a more democratic process when he formally recognised the free tenants and granted them their court in 1297. However, by the latter half of the 16th Century the importance of the English manorial courts had greatly declined, with much of the work they had previously undertaken being dealt with by quarter sessions. For the people of Sheffield, a court appearance now meant a journey into the West Riding.

COURTS AND GAOLS

The justice of the peace, or magistrate, is an old-established figure in English criminal history. The title first appears in a statute of 1361 and traditionally justices were chosen from the knights, esquires and gentlemen of the county.

The justice's principal duty was to inquire into cases brought by the parish constable. Upon arrest, a suspected person was taken before a justice for questioning. The object of this was to obtain a confession and the use of torture in such situations was common in the 16th and 17th Centuries. Once the accused person had confessed, the justice could either deal with him summarily, order him to be whipped or put in the stocks for instance, or he could defer the case to the West Riding Quarter Sessions or York Assizes. The West Riding Sessions were held by the justices at Doncaster, Barnsley, Pontefract, Wakefield and, on occasions, Rotherham. Sheffield did not hold Quarter Sessions until 1880.

An appearance at the sessions was, for many, preceded by a spell in custody at Wakefield House of Correction, opened following an Act of Parliament in 1611 which ordered each county to build such an establishment to set rogues and idle persons to work. Each township contributed towards building and maintenance costs and the magistrates had the responsibility of appointing a governor. In 1641 it was stated at the Quarter Sessions that the governor, Thomas Somerset, was "four score years and upwards" and no longer able to attend the sessions. The court appointed his son to replace him. A year earlier the House of Correction had suffered considerable damage at the hands of soldiers, passing through the town on their way to Selby.

In an age when many crimes went undetected, the law compensated by the severity of punishments imposed for what were often, by modern standards, trifling offences. Nowhere was this more evident than in those cases involving offences against the rights of property which came up before the justices in quarter sessions.

On 11th October, 1637, at Doncaster, John Walker, a labourer of Ecclesfield, was charged with grand larceny – theft of a bible worth 5/-. At the same court, Richard Creswicke, a goldsmith of Sheffield, faced a similar charge involving a riding coat said to be worth 10/-. The charge of grand larceny – the theft of personal property or goods valued at 12d or more – carried the death penalty and, hardly surprisingly, both Walker and Creswicke pleaded not guilty. As often happened in such cases, the sessions jury found both accused guilty of petit larceny by reducing the value of the property stolen – in the case of the riding coat to 10d. Their lives spared, Walker and Creswicke were merely ordered to be "whipped upon the naked body until the blood flows, and then set at large."

Such sentences were common. John Silvester, of Pitsmoor, described as a labourer, was ordered to be whipped at Barnsley sessions in 1640 for stealing half a peck of wheat and rye, valued at 4d. There were many similar cases, with occasional inconsistencies like that of John Chadwicke, accused at Rotherham of breaking into a house and stealing £5 worth of goods. He was fined 2/6d.

One method by which a felon convicted of all but the most serious crimes, such as treason, could avoid the gallows was by claiming he was a member of holy orders. Known as pleading Benefit of Clergy, this loophole was successfully employed at Barnsley in 1638 by Henry Illingworth, a Sheffield man. The criterion for holy orders was literacy – the prisoner was given a bible and told to read verse one of Psalm fifty-one. If he managed this to the satisfaction of the chaplain present then he was spared the death penalty and instead the letter T – for thief – was branded with a red-hot iron on the brawn of his left hand. Such was Illingworth's fate, having pleaded Benefit of Clergy after admitting stealing four lambs.

It is improbable that a labourer like Henry Illingworth would have been literate. What is likely is that he learned to recite the verse – known as the 'Neck Verse' – while in the House of Correction, or that he bribed the chaplain to whisper the words to him. Both tactics were regularly employed during this period, to such a degree that in 1705 the 'Neck Verse' was abandoned, although Benefit of Clergy continued for some time afterwards.

Other common offences against the rights of property were those which contravened the game laws. As landowners themselves, the justices took a stern view of the lower classes roaming their estates in pursuit of rabbits, pheasants and deer. But while offenders convicted of larceny tended to be sentenced to physical punishment, those charged under the game laws at the West Riding Quarter Sessions usually suffered financially.

A typical case was that of Henry Earnshawe and William Radcliffe, both husbandmen from Treeton, who were charged at Barnsley in 1638 with breaking and entering the close of Sir Francis Fane J.P., known as Hell Mother Hill, at Aughton, and hunting a doe with a greyhound. They were each fined 20/-.

Shortly afterwards, at Pontefract, nine Bradfield men were fined a total of £22 for killing six hares. The offence had been committed in February, when snow lay on the ground; the men had traced the hares' footprints in the snow and set two greyhounds on them. It cost each of them more than a year's wages.

Cases of deer-stealing were always committed from the Quarter Sessions to York Assizes. The large number of deer parks at this time provided great temptation: John Harrison's Survey of Sheffield in 1637 estimated that Sheffield Park, an area of 2461 acres, contained 1000 fallow and 200 antler deer. In 1661 George Dickinson was convicted of stealing deer there and around the same time three Sheffield men, including Henry Bright, described as a gentleman, were convicted of killing a stag in Rivelin Forest, owned by the Earl of Arundel. The sentence for offences such as these was three months imprisonment. However, release could only be obtained if sureties for seven years good behaviour were found, and damages were paid to the aggrieved party. Consequently many deer thieves remained in prison indefinitely.

By contrast with the harsh punishments imposed by magistrates for offences against property, everyday violence was treated very leniently. The West Riding Quarter Sessions records show numerous cases of assault from Sheffield, with defendants being frequently fined smaller amounts than those imposed by the Manorial Court for similar offences two hundred years earlier. The exception was if the victim happened to be a bailiff, constable or other official. In a case of assault on the constable of Thorne in the execution of his office, his assailant was fined £3/6/8d.

One of the more colourful characters to go before the West Riding Quarter Sessions was Elizabeth Helliwell. A servant, described at Barnsley Sessions as "a woman of lewd life and conversation", she was accused of attempting to poison her master, Nicholas Spademan, and his wife, by putting rat's bain into their pottage. The magistrates committed her to the Wakefield House of Correction but before she could be taken she was rescued from the constable's custody by a man named William Oates. She escaped, while Oates was captured and sent to York Castle. The following year Elizabeth Helliwell appeared again in the Sessions lists, when she was accused at Barnsley of stealing a hat, waistcoat and apron. She was recorded 'At Large'.

Allowing a prisoner to escape was a serious offence, with costly repercussions for the negligent custodian. On occasions, if he was called away on urgent business, such as pursuing a hue and cry, the constable would commit a recently arrested prisoner to an able-bodied member of the parish to be kept safe and secure until he returned. This responsibility must have been undertaken with some reluctance. One prisoner committed by the constable of Bradfield to the safe-keeping of Richard Worrall escaped, and Worrall was fined £5 at the next Sessions.

Vagrancy in this period was treated with no more tolerance than it had been in earlier centuries. Thomas Garland, an Attercliffe husbandman who had been found begging in Wakefield, was ordered in 1638 to be "burnt on the left shoulder with a Roman R." The court was told that he had "no art, mystery, nor merchandise" whereby he could gain his livelihood. A different type of public nuisance was Thomas Denton of Heeley-cum-Ecclesall. A blacksmith, he pleaded guilty to being a common barrator, a disturber of the peace and an oppressor of his neighbours. Seven witnesses gave evidence against him and he was fined £10. Inability to pay such a fine led to imprisonment for an indefinite period.

Not surprisingly, the justices came in for strong criticism. Their comfortable lifestyles at a time of great poverty and the punitive sentences they so often imposed made them very unpopular with the lower classes. In the West Riding none was more despised than Sir Francis Wortley, knight and baronet, whose Wortley Park was the scene of much illicit hunting which resulted in prosecution and punishment.

Thomas Beale and Walter Hurt were two men who found expressing their opinions of Wortley to be costly. Beale, a pedlar who lived at Masborough, near Rotherham, informed his parish constable that he cared "not a fart" for Sir Francis and would go before neither him nor Mr. Rockley – Robert Rockley Esq., another of the West Riding justices. He went before the Doncaster Sessions in 1639, which included Rockley, and was fined 20/-. Walter Hurt, a Bradfield yeoman, declared on April Fools Day of the same year: "I care not a fart for Sir Francis." He was fined 40/-.

One man whom the magistrates did not have the satisfaction of punishing was James Parkin, an Ecclesfield yeoman. Parkin was recorded 'At Large' when charged with uttering "scandalous, malicious and contemptuous words" about Sir Francis Wortley. He had said, "I worship him with my arse." Such sentiments were undoubtedly shared by many with less courage, or more wisdom, than to utter them publicly.

Magistrates sitting in quarter sessions were empowered to try every type of case with the one exception of high treason. In practice certain other types of offence were also deferred to the twice-yearly Assizes at York, with the accused held in the Castle Gaol until his or her case came up.

The horrors of York Gaol were renowned even in the 13th Century. In 1295 Edward I expressed concern about conditions there as many prisoners had died and those who remained were considered to be in great danger. Starvation and disease were rife and in 1328 a prisoner was fastened to the bare ground by two pairs of irons for three days. He had been imprisoned as a result of a dispute involving land, rather than for any criminal act.

In 1658 the gaol was in such a state of dereliction that the County of York was admonished at the Assizes for the failure to undertake maintenance. By 1677 the gaol was almost in ruins, the work still not having been done, but it remained in use.

Men and women were herded together in cells without light or ventilation, with all manner of depravities and brutalities taking place. Periodic flooding from the River Ouse left parts of the gaol under water. Prisoners were tortured with irons and screws and all were at the mercy of the gaolers for food, which was sold to them at extortionate prices. Those with money could buy privileges; those without starved and, all too often, died.

A court ordering a person to be imprisoned after conviction did not pass sentence for a specified period. At each Assize the number of prisoners was reviewed by a judge, and lessened either by releasing a number or by selling a batch off to the highest bidder.

Many of the people subjected to this existence had committed no crime; they were imprisoned simply because of their religious or political beliefs. An item in the Town Trustees accounts for 1592 shows the Sheffield constable, Thomas Yowle, receiving 5/- for "bearing a papist to York", and during the reigns of Elizabeth I and James I large numbers of Roman Catholics from all parts of Yorkshire, including Sheffield, were sent to York Castle. Incarcerated with thieves and murderers, they were forced to attend services at the Minster, where the Archbishop preached at them. If they protested they were gagged.

By an order of Assize in 1618, magistrates were instructed to ensure that the law was executed against those who absented themselves from divine service, "be they either papists, puritans, idle or loose people." These recusants, as they were known, were subjected to constant scrutiny and harassment by churchwardens and constables. At Barnsley Sessions in 1642 the West Riding justices ordered the homes of all suspected recusants to be searched and any armour, gunpowder or munitions to be removed. A watch was to be kept for "popishe or seditious books and other reliques of popery."

Anyone who was absent from church for a month or more was considered a recusant, and the parish constable sent a list of them to York once a year. The list for Sheffield for 1665 included six names – two married couples and two widows. The names of one Handsworth couple were also submitted.

Of the many local nonconformists persecuted during this period, James Fisher, Vicar of Sheffield 1646-62, is the most celebrated. Following the restoration of the monarchy, legislation was passed to secure a uniformity of worship and belief throughout the nation. Fisher, a Puritan, refused to take the new oaths and was removed from office. Over the next few years he was arrested and imprisoned in York Castle on a number of occasions. He appeared at Rotherham, Doncaster, Wakefield and Pontefract Quarter Sessions on allegations which, when tested in court, proved difficult to substantiate. On one occasion his accuser was shown to have perjured himself and promptly ran away. Another time the prosecution witness was a drunken clergyman who failed to appear. On another occasion an Attercliffe man, condemned to death in the Castle Gaol for murdering his wife, was reputedly offered a pardon if he would swear treason against the Reverend Fisher. Legend has it that he refused and was hanged. This tale may well be apocryphal for there is no record of a murder case in such circumstances around that time. However, what is certain is that Fisher was continually hounded and the effects of the periods he spent in prison on remand broke his health and led to his death in 1666.

Airing opinions on King or Parliament could also prove hazardous, especially in the turbulent mid-century. In 1650, a Rotherham man, John Purveys, a supporter of the recently executed Charles I, was sent to York Gaol on a charge of sedition. He was alleged to have carried a dagger and two long knives to church, saying that he wore them for the honour of his King and that he hoped to do him more service with them than any Cropp (Roundhead) did the Parliament with his long sword.

With the monarchy restored in 1660 it was critics of the Royalists, rather than Cromwell's supporters, who found themselves in the dock. One was George Parkin, an Attercliffe knife-maker. He was alleged by an informer to have said "A King! We were better off without a King than with one!" The king, he said, would "make us all beggars like to himself" and "before twelve months end we shall see King Charles and his head in a pooke, as his father was." Parkin appeared at York Assizes but evidently met a kindred spirit in the judge, who ordered his acquittal with the comment that he had made use of violent language but there was some sense in a portion of what he said!

The 16th and 17th Centuries saw a steady procession of felons despatched from Sheffield to York. The Burgery accounts show regular payments to the constables for taking those whom the justices of the peace declined to deal with to the Castle Gaol – felons like Henry Morton who was taken to York in 1585 and again in 1590; Nicholas Hibberd, who required an escort of two constables at a cost of 13/4d, instead of the usual 5/-; an unnamed thief who stole two heifers from Mr. Sawersbie of Bridgehouses, and a man named Stevenson who, in 1666 when the town was preoccupied with keeping out plague carriers from nearby Eyam, stole the Church lead (from the present day Sheffield Cathedral).

An interesting item in these accounts is a payment of 14/4d in 1585 to a constable named Hellifield "for and towards the charges of setting forth T. Alcocke into Flanders." Alcocke, a Sheffield man, was a prisoner in York Gaol who was released on the agreement that he went to join English forces fighting in Flanders. In this period many prisoners were similarly released from prison to join up wherever armies were fighting at the time.

Other items in the Burgery and the Constable's accounts refer to serious crime. In 1625 there was a fee of 13/4d paid to Mr. Hepworth, the Coroner, in respect of his duties following the stabbing of Henry Law. Another entry of 12d, for the conveying of Law's (unnamed) attacker to the gaol suggests that he was not committed to York Assizes, but was dealt with by the justices. In 1666 a Widow Wright was murdered by a man named John Shore. An entry in the accounts shows a fee of 15/8d paid to Edward Roberts for going to York to prosecute Shore, whose fate is unfortunately not recorded.

A particularly gruesome murder, described in a deposition taken by Thomas Garnett J.P., at Hatfield House, Ecclesfield in 1665, resulted from an argument over pieces of wood. John Burrowes, an apothecary, killed John Jones with an iron bill-hook. A local sheather who was passing by was called to the scene by Jones' wife and saw Burrowes "hewing and hacking" at his victim's throat as he lay dying, and ordering him to lie still. Committed to York Assizes, Burrowes admitted the murder but was acquitted on the grounds of lunacy and set free.

The first reference to guns being used in local crime occurs during this period. In 1640 Zachariah and James Parkin, both of Ecclesfield, were sent to York Gaol from Rotherham Quarter Sessions for forcible entry into a house, where the occupants were assaulted with "a drawne sworde, a staffe and a gunne."

The siege of a house at the Brushes, close to the present-day Firth Park, in 1646, indicates the state of lawlessness in the area at the time. Late in the night of Saturday, 13th June, the house, occupied by a yeoman, Thomas Warter, was visited by a group of unknown men who tried to break in. Two bullets from a musket were fired through the door, narrowly missing Warter's wife and two servants who were sitting by the fire. The following night there was another attempted break-in when a shot was fired through a parlour window, hitting a bed where Mrs. Warter usually slept. A week later two more bullets were fired into the house and during the next month four more assaults were made, on occasions up to five men being present. One night a man got his arm through the door but was wounded by one of the servants wielding a sword. At this stage two of the men were recognised as Thomas Newton and Lawrence Wade. Both were sent to York Castle by William West J.P.

Riotous assemblies were frequent in the 1640s, with cases from Sheffield and Ecclesfield usually resulting in fines for the participants at the Quarter Sessions. In 1674, however, at a time of general discontent over the price of corn, unruliness broke out on a much greater scale when a crowd of about a hundred entered the Corn Market and several shops in the town. Peck and half-peck measures were smashed in an attempt to force traders to give more value for money. Several of the crowd, which numbered many apprentices, were put in the stocks by the constables but were soon rescued by their friends.

A week after this incident a crowd of around three hundred gathered and roamed the streets, threatening to break all new measures on the next market day. Sir John Reresby J.P. rode to Sheffield from his home at Thrybergh, near Rotherham, and with assistance quelled the impending riot. In his memoirs he later wrote: "by binding some of the known leaders to their good behaviour and securing others we discouraged the rest from any further attempt that day." Five people were subsequently imprisoned for their part in this incident.

Reresby's memoirs, while keen to condemn the unruly "rabble", as he termed the Sheffield protesters, suggest that his own conduct, and that of his magisterial ancestor, Sir Thomas Reresby, was far from exemplary on occasions. Relating a dispute at Rotherham Sessions in 1599, over a prisoner who had escaped from the stocks, Sir Thomas addressed Sir William Wentworth: "A turd in thy teeth! Thou art a rascal, a villain and darrest not draw a sword!" He then hit his fellow justice in the face and pulled his ears until they bled. Servants quickly drew their daggers and the rest of the justices had a struggle keeping the peace in the court. Sir

Thomas Reresby was later fined £1000 in the Star Chamber at Westminster, but he never paid. When James I took the throne he obtained the King's pardon and, although he was removed from the bench, he remained Deputy Lieutenant of the County.

In 1682, also at Rotherham, it was Sir John Reresby who caused uproar, at a dinner given by the Duke of Norfolk for the justices attending the Quarter Sessions. During an argument with fellow magistrate Francis Jessop, a supporter of the dissenters and a friend of the ejected vicar, James Fisher, Reresby threw a lead ink-stand at Jessop, cutting his cheek. Both drew their swords but the company intervened before further wounds could be inflicted. Sir John Reresby later wrote, "I was sorry for this incident but provocation could not be overlooked." One can only speculate as to whether he applied the same ideals to those who appeared before him in court.

Of all the recorded executions at York in the centuries before 1700, only four were associated with Sheffield. The first, in 1579, was Charles de Pascal, aged thirty-eight, executed for breaking into a warehouse and stealing silks and drapery goods valued at one hundred guineas. In 1598 Robert Thomas Swedier was hanged for stealing twenty-four guineas and the attempted murder of a Knaresborough man. After execution Swedier's body was taken from the gallows to Knaresborough Forest where it was hung in chains.

Charles Beaumond, in 1607, became the only Sheffield man known to be executed for high treason. Convicted at the Assizes of counterfeiting gold guineas, he was said to "evince striking marks of penitence." Counterfeiting and clipping the edges of coins of the realm was regarded as the most serious crime of the medieval age, hence the charge of high treason. As far back as 1134 it was costing the nation so much that Henry I ordered that all clippers should lose their right hands and testicles. Such measures did little to curb the practice, however, for by the 17th Century clipping and counterfeiting was so widespread that coinage was in great confusion and short supply, with many coins worth barely half their nominal value.

The last man from Sheffield to be hanged at York in the 17th Century was Thomas Empson, twenty-seven, for his part in a highway robbery near Huddersfield. The highwayman is a much glamourised figure in English criminal history, none more so than John Nevison, whose exploits were reputedly the basis for the legend of Dick Turpin's ride from London to York. Nevison and his gang, based at Newark, were known to be responsible for several hold-ups in the Rotherham and Doncaster areas. In 1683 a woman named Elizabeth Burton, the lover of Edward Bracey – a notorious highwayman in his own right and a member of Nevison's gang – was arrested after visiting friends in Sheffield, and charged with stealing clothes. Examined by Sir John Reresby she turned informant on the gang, telling of various robberies including £200 taken from a Rotherham man at Maltby and £30 from a butcher on Rotherham Fair day. Nevison was subsequently arrested in a public house near Wakefield and was hanged, blind drunk, at York in 1684.

The 17th Century was a period of great turbulence. Political and religious upheaval, wars, food shortages and epidemics resulted in large numbers of the population living in acute poverty. By the turn of the century most of the wealthy burgers of Sheffield had moved to live outside the town boundaries and a survey of the town in 1615 revealed that out of a total of 2207 people, 725 were "begging poor" – not able to exist without the charity of their neighbours. Of the remainder, it was estimated that 160 would be reduced to a similar state by less than a fortnight's sickness and 1222 were children and servants – living on small wages and "constrained to work sore." Only a hundred were able to provide any help to others and of these it was estimated that no more than ten had enough ground of their own to keep one cow. Such poverty, together with the resentment engendered by the restrictions on free speech and liberty of conscience, and the violence which prevailed at every level of society, could hardly fail to lead to crime. The surprise is, perhaps, that so little of the crime which reached the courts was of a really serious nature.

BLOOD MONEY

The local historian, R. E. Leader, in his book *Sheffield in the Eighteenth Century* wrote: "The moral sense of the English people was deplorably low, and the Sheffield populace were no better than the rest." The *Sheffield Iris*, looking back in 1830 on conditions in the town eighty years earlier, commented: "General habits on the whole were disgustingly rude and revolting. Children were sent out into the streets for all purposes while some of the jennils, twickets and backsides were too bad to be endured or even described. Brawls among women were frequent, as was child-beating, wife-beating and profane swearing."

It was in this century, in Sheffield, that John Lees, a steel-burner, sold his wife to Samuel Hall, a fellmonger, for 6d. She was delivered up in the Market Place with a halter round her neck. Such arrangements were not uncommon; as late as 1822, in another local transaction, the vendor received five shillings, a silver watch and a gold chain, while the lady concerned was reported as being "nothing loth to the transfer."

Local fairs and feasts were, according to Leader, "opportunities for unbridled orgies" while an old right to whip dogs found at large in the streets was pursued with enthusiasm. For recreation the populace armed themselves with large whips and, seeking out stray dogs, beat them from street to street and often to death.

All classes indulged in bull-baiting, bear-baiting, dog-fighting and cock-fighting. Cock-fighting in particular attracted large numbers of followers, with contests, known as 'mains', organised between villages and neighbouring towns. To breed a bird that would kill those of his rivals was the ambition of many a man, while large bets were often staked on the outcome of such fights.

Drunkenness, too, was becoming an increasing problem, with the Debtors' Gaol, opened in 1756 in Pudding Lane – now King Street – holding large numbers of men and women imprisoned for ale-house debts. In 1787 there were 161 licensed victuallers in the town and the temptations to drown out the harsher aspects of life must have been great.

Sheffield's first Town Hall, built in 1700 at the corner of the Church Yard, included the first gaol in the town. Situated in the basement of the building, it comprised two cells, the larger six feet square by eight feet high, both of which were devoid of natural light. It was known as Sam Wibberley's Parlour, after the gaoler, and prisoners were kept there while awaiting the preliminary hearing of their cases by the justices. From 1763 onwards the town had a resident justice, the Reverend James Wilkinson of Broom Hall, and five years later he was joined on the bench by John Murray of Banner Cross. Their weekly petty sessions were held first in a room of the Cutlers' Hall and later at the Town Hall. Wilkinson also had a court-room built on to his home. These hearings were held in private; magistrates were not legally obliged to sit in public until 1848.

Minor offences continued to be dealt with summarily by way of fines, the stocks, whipping etc. Whippings were administered by the Town Hall beadle and records refer to men being flogged as they were dragged through the town behind carts. In 1746 two women, named Buck and Clayton, were publicly whipped for stealing linen. The beadle also escorted prisoners to the Wakefield House of Correction. There was no transport; the prisoners walked the whole way, chained together like a slave gang.

Capital crimes increased sharply in 18th Century Sheffield. Between 1766 and 1801 there were fourteen cases from the town which resulted in execution, for offences ranging from the theft of a leg of mutton to brutal murder.

The only differentiation in law between such offences lay in the way the bodies were treated after execution. A person who had killed another was executed within forty-eight hours of conviction and his body given to a medical school for dissection, while the bodies of minor offenders were handed back to their friends for burial. When the crime was considered particularly wicked then the body was hung in chains and, following the Act for Better Preventing of the Horrid Crime of Murder in 1752, the corpses of certain executed criminals were ordered to be gibbeted.

Perhaps the most insidious aspect of the criminal justice system of the period was the payment of money to witnesses who gave evidence which resulted in a conviction. 'Blood money' led to conspiracy, perjury and, in the case of John Stevens and Thomas Lastley, the execution of two young men who had done nothing more than play a joke on a workmate.

Stevens, a single man who lodged in Pinstone Street, and Lastley, who lived with his wife and child in Burgess Street, were button makers. One evening in 1789 they and three workmates, Bingham, Booth and Wharton, were out drinking. Wharton had earlier purchased a backet of groceries, which the others mischievously seized and took to the Barrel Inn, Pinstone Street. Once there they took a leg of mutton from the basket and cooked it, expecting Wharton to join them in eating it, as he knew their intended destination.

However, Wharton did not see the joke, and instead of following his friends to the Barrel he went and complained to the constable, at the time George 'Buggy' Eyre. Despite their explanation, and offer to compensate Wharton for his leg of mutton, Stevens, Lastley, Booth and Bingham were arrested for highway robbery and tried at York Assizes in April, 1790. Bingham was acquitted and the other three condemned to death, although Booth's sentence was soon commuted to transportation for life.

Support for the remaining two condemned men was widespread in Sheffield, with the Master Cutler and many leading townspeople signing a petition which resulted in a reprieve being sent from London to York. Unfortunately for Stevens and Lastley it did not arrive until two days after they had been executed, protesting their innocence – and Wharton's knowledge of it – to the end.

The people of Sheffield, aware that a hundred pounds 'blood money' had been paid, expressed great anger towards Wharton and Constable Eyre. In the meantime Booth had received an unconditional pardon and had returned to Sheffield. To add fuel to the controversy a letter, written by the two unfortunate men the night before they were executed, and protesting an absolute lack of criminal intent, had been made public by their former workmates. The *Sheffield Register* reported "much disturbance has arisen in this town since the execution of Stevens and Lastley, from an idea that the prosecutor swore to aggravated circumstances which really did not happen . . . .The populace have several times beset Wharton's house, and hung the figure of a man on a gibbet before his door, but yesterday they were so violent as to break every window, and otherwise so much damage the house as to render it scarcely habitable." Wharton, disguised in women's clothing, escaped to Manchester and was never seen in Sheffield again.

Another local case in which allegations of 'blood money' were prominent was that of John Hoyland. A seventy-seven year old Attercliffe man, Hoyland was charged with bestiality after two labourers, John Hurt and William Warburton, swore on oath that they had witnessed him having intercourse with an ass. Hoyland totally denied the charge and all who knew him believed him to be an innocent victim of perjury, but he was nonetheless hanged at York in 1793.

Burglaries in Sheffield accounted for three executions during this period. The first was that of Isaac Turner, hanged at York in front of a large crowd in 1766 for stealing goods from two dwelling houses in the Market Place. A woman, Lydia Nicholson, charged with receiving the goods, was acquitted; female accomplices were often acquitted by juries unwilling to see them hang.

In 1786, two labourers, William Sharp and William Bamford, both in their twenties, were hanged for breaking into the house of Duncan McDonald, a Sheffield button maker, and stealing a number of horn combs, a silver threepenny piece and fourpence in copper.

Shop-breaking also attracted the ultimate penalty. On April 17th, 1790, the same day as Stevens and Lastley met their untimely end, and on the same scaffold, George Moore, a well known prize fighter from Sheffield's Park district, was executed for breaking into a York shop. He was in the town, having enlisted with the 19th Foot Regiment in Sheffield and returned with them to their headquarters. Moore – known as 'Docky' – was noted for his exploits in the ring. He fought an epic battle on Crookes Moor with a man named Dewsnap and his defeat at the hands of Bill Richmond, the black American, on York racecourse was chronicled by Piers Egan in his classic work on the history of pugilism, *Boxiana*, published in 1812. From his death cell Moore wrote to his father in Sheffield, asking to see him before he died and a public subscription raised enough money to send the old man, who had appeared extremely upset about the fate of his son, to York.

Moore senior embarked on his journey but only got as far as Brightside – a distance of three miles – when he got drunk on the money and returned home, telling his friends that he could have done no good for his son if he had seen him.

Highway robbery was, for some, a lucrative business, the gains making the risks worthwhile. John Vickers, who committed two robberies on the same dark Saturday night in February, 1775, was clearly not in this class. In the first, near to the Blue Ball, Attercliffe, he assaulted a man named John Murfin and relieved him of 3½d in copper, a bad shilling, a breast of mutton and half a pound of butter tied up in a handkerchief. Later, close to the Glass House, and with an accomplice, he robbed his former master, John Staniforth, of 3/6d, a sacking wallet, a leg of mutton, six pounds of sugar and some flax. Identified by his victims, Vickers went to the gallows while his accomplice was acquitted.

The most brutal local crime during the 18th Century was undoubtedly the murder of Nathan Andrews, a jeweller with a shop in the High Street. Andrews was found lying in a field at Kirk Edge, near Bradfield, on March 19th, 1782. His head had been savagely battered, he had stab wounds to the stomach and his throat was cut.

His killer was Frank Fearn, a man in his early twenties who had been recently sacked from his apprenticeship as a file-maker because of his drinking and petty thieving. Fearn had lured Andrews to his death on the pretext that he was the treasurer of a watch club at Bradfield. Watch and clock clubs were very popular among workmen at the time. Twenty or so formed a club, usually based in a public house, appointed a treasurer and contributed a few pence each week. In their turn each obtained a watch from the funds and it was usual for jewellers or watchmakers to occasionally attend the clubs and show their wares. Thus Fearn called upon Andrews at his shop and the latter agreed to take a number of watches to a club which Fearn claimed was held at The Horns, Bradfield.

The pair set off to walk to their destination and, at a conveniently isolated spot, Fearn drew a knife and killed the jeweller. Once the body was discovered he was soon suspected, as Andrews had told his wife with whom he was travelling, and Fearn was arrested in bed at his lodgings in Sims Croft. He immediately admitted that he was the murderer and a watch belonging to the victim was found in his room.

Initially locked up at the Town Hall, Fearn was tried and convicted at York Assizes in July, 1782. Despite the serious nature of the charge he was not legally represented and the trial judge, Sir James Eyre, in sentencing him to death, ordered that his body should be gibbeted "on some conspicuous spot" on Loxley Common.

Fearn was executed on July 23rd. He is reputed to have taken off his shoes on the scaffold and flung them to the crowd, declaring that his former master had always said he would die with his shoes on and he wished to make him a liar! His body was gibbeted soon afterwards and the last of his bones did not fall to the ground until Christmas, 1797. The gibbet post was taken down in the early years of the following century.

Spence Broughton has a unique place in Sheffield history as the only criminal to have a road named after him. Broughton Lane, lying between Attercliffe Common and Tinsley Park Road, begins close to the spot where the mail robber's gibbet stood for more than thirty years.

Broughton was born into a wealthy Lincolnshire family around the middle years of the eighteenth century. After a good education he married a young woman who brought with her a dowry of £1500 and he settled down to a comfortable life as a farmer. But the delights of horse-racing, bull-running and cock-fighting proved a strong attraction and he soon deserted his wife and children for the cockpits of Sheffield, Grantham and Derby.

Having lost several thousand pounds, Broughton struck up a partnership with a man named John Oxley, a former stable boy at Wentworth House. Oxley was deeply involved in cock-fighting and as a result of several shady transactions soon became obliged to leave the area. The pair moved to London but in February, 1791 they returned – for the specific purpose of robbing the Sheffield to Rotherham mail.

The *Sheffield Advertiser* of February 4th, 1791 reported: "On Saturday night as the post-boy between Sheffield and Rotherham was riding with the mail he was attacked near the latter place by a man who, after leading his horse a little way from the road, pulled the boy off, blindfolded him with a handkerchief, tied his hands behind him, then cut the straps by which the bag was fastened, and ran off with it. The offender has not yet been found or even heard of, but on Monday the bag was found near Aughton, containing part of the letters."

The robbery took place at Ickles, on the Rotherham edge of Attercliffe Common. The post-boy, George Leasley, after wriggling out of his bonds and removing his blindfold, found his horse tied to a nearby gate and was able to ride on unharmed.

Eight months later, in October, John Oxley was arrested in a public house in London on suspicion of changing banknotes stolen from the King's Mail in a robbery at Cambridge the previous June. As a result of Oxley's arrest, Broughton was also caught when he visited the house of Thomas Shaw, a known receiver. Confronted by John Townsend, the well known Bow Street Runner, Broughton took to his heels and was only captured after a hectic chase through the City streets. He had bills and banknotes worth £3000 in his possession.

When Oxley appeared in court at Bow Street he made a full confession of his activities as a highway robber, admitting the Cambridge and Attercliffe hold-ups, and another at Aylesbury in May. He implicated Broughton to the full, as did the receiver, Thomas Shaw, who it soon became clear had been seriously involved in plotting the robberies.

Shaw had negotiated the cashing of some of the bills after the Cambridge robbery, which produced a haul estimated at over £5000. Assured by officers of the Crown that his life would be safe if he told all he knew, he turned King's Evidence.

Shaw had suggested the Attercliffe robbery to Broughton and Oxley, knowing that they were familiar with the area. He had advanced them ten guineas each to help them on their way but the pair had been unable to get seats on the London-Sheffield coach and had walked much of the way, riding in carriers' wagons when they had the opportunity.

On arrival in Sheffield they spent the night at an inn before walking across Lady's Bridge and along Attercliffe Common. There, Broughton, who kept a stock of disguises at his London lodgings, changed into a smock and an old hat and they awaited the mail. When it arrived Broughton stopped the post-boy and, having stolen the mail bag, they hurried away, walking to Mansfield where they put up at a public house. To Broughton's dismay they had only secured one worthwhile item, a bill for £123 drawn on a London merchant and payable to a Rotherham man. They burned the remainder of the mail and Oxley hurried to London by coach to cash the bill, while Broughton, who was exhausted, stayed in Mansfield to recover and travelled on later.

Following his arrest Broughton was locked up in Newgate Prison, while Shaw and Oxley went to Tothill Fields and Clerkenwell Prisons respectively. However, Oxley did not remain long behind bars, escaping in extremely suspicious circumstances at 7 pm one evening, never to be seen or heard of again. As Shaw had gone over to the prosecution, Broughton alone now faced the serious charges and, since the Attercliffe robbery was the clearest case against him, he was removed from Newgate to York Castle to await trial at the Spring Assizes.

Broughton's trial lasted less than two hours. The principal witnesses for the prosecution were Shaw and a man named John Close, who kept one home and wife in Change Alley, Sheffield and another in London, where he ran a lottery office and gaming tables in partnership with Shaw. Close corroborated the latter's evidence and this proved damning to Broughton who, so it was reported, said little during the proceedings.

Mr. Justice Buller, in passing sentence, declared that the crime which Broughton had committed was most baneful to society and was of such a character as to leave him without a shadow of hope that he could receive any mercy this side of the grave. In order to deter others it was necessary that his punishment should not cease at the place of execution, but that his body should afterwards be suspended between earth and Heaven – as unworthy of either – to be buffeted about by the winds and storms. He then passed sentence of death and advised Broughton to make best use of the little time he had left.

Three weeks later, on April 14th, 1792, Spence Broughton was hanged along with four burglars whose collective plunder did not amount to a guinea. As so often happened with this method of execution, he 'died hard', convulsive struggles occurring for six or seven minutes after the rope tightened on his neck. Later the same day his body was removed and transported to Sheffield, where the gibbet had been erected in readiness on Attercliffe Common. It arrived on the 16th to a scene of great excitement and a carnival atmosphere which continued for weeks to come. On the first day an estimated 40,000 people turned out on the Common and the landlord of the nearest pub, The Arrow, frequently stated in later years that whatever harm Broughton did to others, he had certainly helped him make a fortune.

As late as 1817 Broughton's bones could still be seen and the tattered remains of his clothes still blew in the wind. The gibbet, thought to be the last set up in Yorkshire, was finally taken down in 1827, when, following the Enclosure Acts, the then owner of the field in which it stood grew tired of curious trespassers clambering over his hedges and ditches to get a closer look.

Spence Broughton's fate aroused a considerable amount of sympathy from the Sheffield public, whose anger and suspicions about 'blood money' were revived by Shaw turning informer and Oxley's mysterious escape from prison. Broughton, however, faced death without complaint. On the scaffold, in clear and unfaltering tones, he addressed the vast crowd, saying he had been a great offender and the sentence passed upon him was just, and asking those who had assembled to see him die to pray for his departing soul. No doubt such fortitude served to enhance the legend.

SCENES OF GREAT DISORDER

Riots occurred in many counties of England during the eighteenth century. Throughout the country, and especially in the second half of the century, there were uprisings against the introduction of turnpikes, machinery and enclosures, and violent protests about increasing food prices. At Leeds in 1753 a mass rising of people from the surrounding towns and villages against the levies being raised at toll gates was put down by armed force. At Limehouse the wrecking of a mechanical saw-mill was quickly followed by the 1769 Riot Act[1], which made the wilful destruction of any building containing machinery a capital offence. Disturbances in many towns resulted in the seizure of grain and flour from shops and mills and at Kidderminster, in such an incident, eight men were killed.

Commenting on the period in Sheffield, R. E. Leader wrote: "If not viciously criminal beyong the average . . . . the Sheffielders were yet a turbulent race, very apt, whether with or without reason, to express their feelings by rioting."

The Sheffield public had shown that they would not willingly accept increases in the price of food when they rebelled in Sir John Reresby's day. The middle years of the 18th Century saw further rises in the cost of necessities and the populace once again rose up in protest. Over a four day period in August 1756 the town was in a state of considerable chaos. One account describes "the mob carrying all before them and breathing nothing but fury and destruction."

Magistrates were summoned and the Marquis of Rockingham, together with Mr. Battie J.P., came to the town and recruited ten new constables. R. E. Leader quotes a contemporary letter, written August 28th: "A very good scheme was formed by raising a company of stout, able men, who assembled last night well armed with bludgeons, guns and bayonets, knocked down all before them they knew to be of the gang of the mob, patrolled the town round and seized all the ringleaders, some in bed, some in the streets." Thirty people were taken before the magistrates and subsequently imprisoned in York Castle.

An increase in the price of coal led to disturbances in the town in 1728. The local colliery owner, the eighth Duke of Norfolk, instructed his agent to raise the price 1/2d per pack-horse load. At the same time he proposed to repair the road from pit to town, thinking this would meet with popular approval. His error of judgement led to the first riots of the century in Sheffield.

---

[1]The first Riot Act was passed in 1714. It was a means of ordering crowds to disperse and anyone present one hour after it had been read aloud by a J.P. could be arrested. It was not repealed until 1967.

The ninth Duke, in 1774, decided to improve the method of transporting coal from the colliery to the town. A tramway of wooden rails, two miles long, was laid from the colliery, which lay at the highest part of the Park – close to Manor Castle – down to the bottom of Park Hill, the old junction of South Street and Broad Street. Coal was conveyed in large wagons which ran along the tramway.

Local carters, however, seeing the threat to their occupation, spread rumours that the laying of the tramway was to lead to an increase in the price of coal and in the subsequent riot the tramway and loading stage were burned. Several wagons were destroyed and one was set on fire and pushed into the river. A man named Shaw was struck by a constable and died soon afterwards, while the mob proceeded to the Lord's House in Fargate, dispersing only after soldiers arrived and shots were fired.

The Acts of Parliament of the late 18th Century which resulted in the enclosure of common land were very unpopular with the majority of the population. From time immemorial wastes and commons had been used for sport and recreation, for picking fruit, cutting wood and grazing animals.

Thus the enclosure of Little Sheffield Moor and Crookes Moor, where Sheffield Races were held until 1781, annoyed many local people and on July 29th, 1791 a mob assembled outside the Tontine Inn in the Haymarket, moving to King Street where the Debtors' Gaol was stormed and all the prisoners liberated. The mob then marched on to Broom Hall, home of Reverend Wilkinson, Vicar of Sheffield and the town's first resident magistrate. Haystacks were fired, windows broken, and damage inflicted to furniture and the library. The mob was dispersed by the arrival of a company of dragoons, called from Nottingham.

Five men were arrested and committed to York. Four of these – Furness, Johnson, Froggatt and Ellis – were later released, while the fifth, John Bennett, was found guilty and hanged on September 2nd, 1791. Bennett was a young man of low intelligence and once again allegations of 'blood money' and perjury abounded, the common belief being that he had been the unwitting scapegoat for others.

Leader ascribes the causes of the 1791 riot not only to local enclosures but also to long-standing resentment about standards of justice and punishment. The Reverend Wilkinson, who, on a later occasion had a small girl placed in the stocks for reciting an innocuous rhyme about him, was an obvious target for such resentment. The knowledge that he had purchased several acres of enclosed land served only to increase antagonism towards him.

Wilkinson was subsequently reimbursed by the town in the sum of £190 for the damage to his furniture and library. He claimed a further £409 for the eight haystacks which had been destroyed. One effect of the riot was a decision to build barracks at Hillsborough, with accommodation for two hundred cavalry. In an era of unrest the town authorities had become aware of the need to have means of suppression close at hand.

Reverend James Wilkinson. Sheffield's first resident magistrate. Photo: Sheffield City Libraries.

The following year, on May 4th, 1792, another incident occurred outside the Tontine Inn. Several people were wounded and windows of the inn were broken when the military were called to disperse a crowd protesting about low wages and the enclosures.

The state of tension which existed in Sheffield at this time was attributed by the authorities to the influence of Tom Paine, whose *Rights of man* was said to be familiar to the local populace. The effects of the French Revolution, which had begun in 1789, were felt throughout Britain and Sheffield was no exception. Public meetings were held to petition for peace and an extension of the voting franchise and in 1794 James Montgomery, editor of the *Sheffield Iris*, was imprisoned for three months for publishing a song considered libellous towards the King and his conduct in the war with France.

Colonel Robert Athorpe J.P. Unpopularly known as 'Beef-Headed Bob'.
Photo: Sheffield City Libraries

In 1795 a military revolt in Sheffield left two dead and many others seriously wounded. A Colonel Cameron had recruited, at his own expense, a Sheffield Regiment of Foot from the ranks of the unemployed. He intended to place them at the service of the government but on August 7th a dispute broke out on the parade ground in Norfolk Street when the men refused to march without an advance of money. A crowd quickly gathered and joined in the dispute which soon became a scene of great disorder. Another newly raised regiment, the Sheffield Loyal Independent Volunteers, were called and their colonel, Robert Athorpe J.P., rode immediately from his home near Rotherham. He read the Riot Act, to no avail, and ordered his men to fire. At the subsequent inquest on the fatalities verdicts of justifiable homicide were recorded.

Athorpe, an unpopular figure locally – he was known as 'Beef-Headed Bob' – was a regular companion of the Reverend Wilkinson on the magistrates' bench. He had been made colonel of the Volunteers only a short time before the Norfolk Street riot and appears to have been rather over-zealous in his reaction to the incident. Contemporary accounts of his conduct are conflicting. The Tory *Courant* said that he rode about asking people to disperse. The *Iris* stated that he "plunged with his horse among the unarmed, defenceless people, and wounded with his sword men, women and children promiscuously." The latter report led to the editor, James Montgomery, once again finding himself in York Castle Gaol, this time for six months, having been convicted of libelling Athorpe.

One of the leading protagonists in many of the disturbances of this period was John Blackwell, a journeyman tailor. Also known as Jacky Blacker, 'King of the Gallery', in May 1812 he was involved in the storming of the Volunteers' arms depot in Spital Hill by a mob of several hundred people. Weapons were removed and smashed while a large gathering of bystanders looked on and once again the military were called. Over the next few months a number of violent protests over food and flour prices erupted and on August 18th a large mob assembled in the town and proceeded to force traders to sell flour at half its previous price.

John Blackwell escaped imprisonment in 1812, although others were not so fortunate. Later that year he led a mass protest against the singing of the national anthem in the theatre. He led the interruptions from the gallery and thus inherited the title 'King of the Gallery', formerly held by the radical poet and thorn-in-the-side of the local authorities, Joe Mather, who had died in 1804.

In 1816 Blackwell led a large demonstration from the Wicker to the Market Place. On the top of a pole he carried a loaf dipped in blood and the slogan 'Bread or Blood' was prominently displayed. The demonstrators had hoped to meet the magistrates and to ask them to ensure that food was sold at reasonable prices, but the situation degenerated into uproar and several shops were destroyed before the Hussars arrived to scatter the crowd. Blackwell was arrested after John Wortley J.P., later the first Lord

Wharncliffe, leaped into the crowd and siezed him. He spent two years in York Gaol.

Shortly after he was released Blackwell became involved in plans for a large uprising which was to take place in Sheffield in Spring 1820. On April 11th he and a few hundred others paraded round the town with weapons, only to be dispersed in the Wicker. Charged with collecting mobs, encouraging others to riot and having in his possession a loaded pistol, a pike and other weapons, he was sentenced to two-and-a-half years imprisonment. When he was released this time, the 'King of the Gallery' was a broken man. He spent much of the remainder of his life in the poorhouse, dying there in 1839, aged fifty-three.

The Reform Act of 1832 extended the right to a parliamentary vote to about 3,500 citizens of Sheffield, out of a total male population of 30,000. The first election following the act took place on December 14th of the same year, and a vast crowd assembled outside the Corn Exchange where the hustings were held. The announcement of the first return of the poll, indicating a victory for John Parker, of Woodthorpe, was greatly unpopular with the crowd, most of whom did not qualify for a vote.

A section of the crowd gathered outside the Tontine Inn, where Parker had held meetings, and began throwing stones and coal at the windows. They then moved on to attack the home of Parker's solicitor, in Bank Street. The Riot Act was read, special constables assembled, and a despatch was sent to Rotherham to summon an infantry regiment which was stationed there.

At 10.15 that evening, after the mob had paraded for over four hours, damaging property and assaulting the constables, the infantry arrived in the form of a detachment of the 18th Irish Foot. With a magistrate, Thomas Bosville, at their head, the soldiers marched up Waingate and took up position in front of the Tontine, whereupon Bosville was promptly struck on the head with a stone. The order was given to fire, the soldiers complied, and very quickly five people lay dead and many more severely wounded. The dead were: George Grimes, of Orchard Street; James Turton, of Wheeldon Street; James Jackson, of Brown Street; and two boys – William Howard, of Lambert Street, and David Ogden, of Eyre Lane – both aged 14. A sixth man, Jesse Fretwell, aged 19, died later in the Infirmary. The Coroner recorded verdicts of justifiable homicide on all the dead.

Throughout the 1830s political unrest festered and spread. The introduction of the workhouse as the only permitted means of relief for the poor, and the decline in the cutlery trade – mainly attributed to a panic on the American financial market – aroused strong feelings among the working classes of Sheffield. In October 1837 the first local Chartist group, the Sheffield Workingmen's Association, was formed. It pledged to obtain universal suffrage, secret ballots and other demands which were expressed nationally in the 'People's Charter', acclaimed at mass meetings throughout the country in 1839. When the Government failed to be persuaded, and following disturbances in other towns when police and soldiers attacked people gathered at Chartist meetings, activists in Sheffield were urged to take up arms.

A number of meetings were held in Paradise Square and on several Sundays in the autumn of 1839 Chartists occupied the Parish Church in large numbers. Armed police were stationed at the gates to the church yard after a particularly disturbed service on September 8th. Three days later, an Irishman, William Martin, was arrested and charged with sedition after delivering a speech at the Chartists' meeting room in Figtree Lane. Martin was alleged to have said that if any magistrate dare issue a warrant against him or his brothers he would assassinate him, by day or by night. He asked those present: "Is there a man amongst you who cannot make a blade that will draw blood?"

The following day a series of disturbances in the town led to thirty-six arrests. The First Royal Dragoons were called out and when those arrested came up in court a guard was posted round the Town Hall. The accused were either sentenced to short periods of imprisonment or ordered to find sureties to keep the peace.

After the early skirmishes an ambitious plot was hatched to take control of Sheffield by armed force in January 1840. With the support of groups in surrounding towns and villages it was planned to plunder gun shops in the town and to seize the Town Hall and Tontine Inn as headquarters. Men were instructed to set fire to the barracks, to the houses of magistrates, and to kill policemen. Spiked balls were to be scattered in the streets to cripple the cavalrymen's horses and the use of bombs and grenades, which the conspirators had been manufacturing and collecting for some time, figured prominently. The local leaders, headed by Samuel Holberry, an unemployed distiller, hoped that after the initial blows had been struck assistance would be forthcoming from Chartists in other parts of the country.

The plans were foiled when James Allen, a Rotherham publican, turned informer. The uprising never took place, although odd groups gathered and two watchmen were shot and wounded in one struggle. Holberry and his associates were arrested on January 11th and appeared before the magistrates at the Town Hall two days later, charged with high treason. On a table in the courtroom spears, daggers, guns, bombs, hand grenades, cartridges and fireballs were exhibited.

The Sheffield Chartists went on trial at York Spring Assizes in 1840. Such was the importance attached to the case that the prosecution was led by the Attorney General, Sir John Campbell. Found guilty, Samuel Holberry, in whose house at 19, Eyre Lane, bombs had been found, was sentenced to four years imprisonment. Thomas Booker and William Booker, cutlers of

Bennett Lane, received three and two year sentences; James Duffy, a beer house keeper of Spring Street, three years; John Clayton of Porter Street, John Marshall of Coalpit Lane, Thomas Penthorpe of Spring Street and Joseph Bennison of the Park were each sentenced to two years.

Most of the Chartists were sent to Northallerton House of Correction, where conditions were notoriously harsh. Solitary confinement, the rule of silence, the treadmill and picking oakum were the order of the day. John Clayton, who was fifty-five years old, died before he had served a year of his sentence and in June 1842, Samuel Holberry, whose health had rapidly deteriorated through tuberculosis, died at the age of twenty-seven. Holberry became a martyr to the working classes of Sheffield, an estimated 50,000 of whom lined the streets to the General Cemetery for his funeral. The local Chartists did reorganise, but disbanded for good in the 1850s, their aims having been largely achieved. Their leader is commemorated in the Holberry Society, a labour history group formed in Sheffield in 1978.

The next significant disturbances against public order in Sheffield occurred during the miners' strike of 1844, a dispute over wages. When six hundred men came out on strike, the employers brought in unemployed Derbyshire miners to work the Soap House Pit, situated at the lower end of the Park, close to Duke Street.

The strike-breakers were temporarily lodged in buildings within the pit premises and on July 4th, 1844 several hundred strikers assembled at the pit gates. Stones were thrown at the Derbyshire men and threats were uttered to pull out their livers and brains. Despite no serious injury being caused, three Sheffield men, George Taylor, William Mason and Richard Winker, were sentenced to fifteen years transportation when they appeared at York Assizes charged with rioting. Several independent witnesses gave evidence that Taylor was at his lodgings at the time of the disturbance.

The Sheffield populace were always quick to show their sensitivity regarding interference with the remains of the dead. Much controversy occurred in 1785 when the widening of Church Street necessitated the removal of graves, but this was nothing to the outrage fifty years later over the activities of the 'resurrection men'.

These ghoulish individuals, also known as 'stiff lifters', provided the burgeoning medical profession with bodies, which were then used for dissection. The Anatomy Act of 1832 allowed the dissection of paupers in medical schools, but the resurrection men raided any newly interred grave, dug up the body and sold it to the medical school. In Edinburgh the notorious Burke and Hare went one step further by suffocating selected victims and delivering their bodies direct to the schools. This practice became known as 'burking'.

In Sheffield, a medical school, where students learned anatomy, was situated at the corner of Eyre Street and Charles Lane. On January 26th, 1835 a domestic dispute between the caretaker and his wife led to violence, and the wife, thrown into the street, began to shout and scream 'murder'. Passers-by formed the mistaken impression that an attempt had been made to 'burke' the woman in the medical school. The rumour spread quickly and a large crowd gathered. The building was forcibly entered, skeletons and corpses were found, and the crowd set the premises alight. Constables and the fire brigade could not get near the scene for the crowd, which dispersed only with the arrival of the military. However, after two hours the soldiers withdrew and the mob returned to set the building on fire once again. This time it was gutted. No-one was ever successfully prosecuted for the destruction; James Ogden and Thomas Staniforth were tried on a charge of being concerned in the riot but both were acquitted at York Assizes.

Although the cause of the disturbance was seen as drunkenness, superstition and general unruliness among the lower orders, there were widespread feelings of suspicion about the methods medical schools employed to obtain bodies. Even the *Lancet* commented that those inclined to condemn the Sheffield rioters should first recollect the recent activities of Burke.

Interference with the dead did not end with the destruction of the medical school. In 1862 a disturbance occurred at St. Philip's Cemetery, following reports that the sexton was selling bodies for dissection. His house was destroyed by a mob incensed by the discovery of a large hole in the ground, containing open coffins and mutilated remains. The sexton was later imprisoned for three months for disinterring the dead and the Vicar of St. Philip's, the Reverend Livesey, received a three week sentence for falsifying entries in the register.

The riots of the 18th century were precipitated by a number of factors. Rising prices, unpopular legislation and dissatisfaction with the administration of justice all played their part. The 19th Century brought about an increased political awareness among the working classes, reflected in those incidents concerned with the rights of the individual. After the Chartists there was a temporary respite in political and industrial disorder in Sheffield. When it returned, in the 'rattening' outrages which pervaded the grinders' unions from the late 1840s to the 1880s there would once again be violence, destruction and death.

TRANSPORTED BEYOND THE SEAS

In the first half of the 19th Century, national statistics for indictable crime multiplied six times over. In 1805 there were five thousand committals from magistrates' courts; by 1848 the figure was thirty thousand plus. Much of this crime occurred in the larger towns, where social conditions were, for many, extremely poor. Mass migration from country areas, as society changed within a few generations from rural to industrial, led to overcrowding, high mortality rates and exploitation. As the old communities scattered in pursuit of work, so the old values, which had ensured social discipline for generations, were eroded. Increased drunkenness, relative poverty which meant the urban poor could see wealth around them, and the return to civilisation of thousands of soldiers from the Napoleonic Wars – without any hope of work or financial support – brought about an upsurge in criminal activity which was the result of a society in rapid, and violent, transition.

In Sheffield the population grew from 45,755 in 1801 to 135,310 in 1851. The crime rate increased from an 1819 total of 164 felonies (including seven capital offences), to 346 in 1845. In 1850 3,187 people were taken into custody in the town, an increase of twenty per cent on the figures for five years earlier.

Magistrates sat daily in the new Town Hall, the present-day Crown Court building in Castle Street. The new building opened in 1808 when the old Town Hall, at the Church Gates, was demolished. The majority of the petty offences the magistrates dealt with concerned thefts of clothing or food, picking pockets of watches and silk handkerchiefs, shoplifting and assaults.

Fairs continued to attract undesirables in large numbers, so much so that it was thought necessary to publish warning notices. On Saturday, November 29th, 1823 the first page of the *Sheffield Independent* announced:

STOP THIEF!!

The WINTER FAIR always brings to the Town of Sheffield, Thieves, Housebreakers, Pickpockets, Swindlers, Rogues and Vagabonds of every description. The COMMITTEE of the ASSOCIATION for the PROSECUTION of FELONS, &c. therefore take this opportunity of warning the Inhabitants against the Depredators. They also direct attention to the wicked practices of IDLE and DISORDERLY BOYS, many of whom are acquainted with RECEIVERS of STOLEN GOODS; it is hoped that the nefarious trade of the latter will soon meet with a salutary check.

Associations for the Prosecution of Felons, as referred to in this notice, sprang up in hundreds of towns and villages in the country between 1750 and 1856. Formed largely by the propertied classes, they were primarily prosecuting societies, rather than being directly involved in the apprehension of criminals, at a time when the cost and complexities of the legal system resulted in many people refusing to prosecute those who had offended against them. Locally there were associations in Sheffield, Ecclesfield, Bradfield and Norton. The latter, titled the 'Norton Association for the Prosecution of Felons, Receivers of Stolen Goods and Cattle and other Legal Objects', continues in name if not practice to the present day.

During the late 18th and early 19th Centuries so great a number of offences carried capital punishment that there is difficulty in establishing true figures. Prior to the repealing campaigns which gained momentum in the 1820s and resulted in a reduction from over 220 capital offences to only four by 1861, the range of offences for which the death penalty could be ordered ran from murder, burglary and pickpocketing, to sacrilege, treason and returning from transportation, via stealing an heiress, pulling down a house, or cutting down trees in an avenue or garden. But while sentence of death was often pronounced in court, it was frequently later commuted to transportation, an alternative which not only removed criminals from society, but also provided labour for the colonies.

The first transportees were sent to America, under a 1597 'Acte for the Punyshment of Rogues, Vagabonds and Sturdy Beggars', which gave justices the power to banish felons 'beyond the seas'. After the Declaration of Independence in 1776 America refused to accept further consignments and so Australia became the main dumping ground for Britain's convicts.

Between 1788 and 1868 162,000 men, women and children – some as young as nine years old – were transported to Australia and Tasmania. The penal settlements of New South Wales, where those with the longest sentences and worst records were sent, were little better than slave camps. Brutal discipline existed and the lash was used unsparingly.

Letters from John Grayson, alias William Butterworth, to his father in Penistone, near Sheffield, give a first-hand account of convict life. Grayson was transported for life in 1829, having been initially sentenced to death for an attempted bank robbery. He was kept in prison and then on a Thames 'hulk' until sufficient convicts were gathered together to fill a ship. His voyage lasted four months, which was unusually short, seven months being normal passage time, and he arrived in Van Dieman's Land where he was assigned to a farmer.

Grayson wrote: "A prisoner lives bad, lays bad, and is always thought bad upon, and there are some of the worst characters here of any part of the world . . . .If you look wrong they can take you before a magistrate and give you 50 lashes or three months in irons. For the least you ever do there is 25 lashes with a cat o' nine tails."

Other accounts of life in the convict settlements describe instances of men receiving up to three hundred lashes, the flesh reduced to jelly and cut to the bone. The gallows, too, were in frequent use – the execution rate in New South Wales in the 1820s was calculated on a per capita basis as three hundred times higher than in Britain.

Many offenders from Sheffield were transported. Some were extremely fortunate to be escaping the gallows, in view of the serious nature of their crimes, while others' transgressions, committed out of desperation and poverty, would today warrant only the mildest sentence.

In the first category was William Smith, a fifteen year old apprentice at Gallimore's Wheel. On January 22nd, 1833 a grinder named Whiteley visited the wheel, looking for work. A quarrel arose between the visitor and Smith, which soon developed into a fight, and Smith, getting the worst of it, picked up a scissor blade and stabbed Whiteley. With his bowels protruding he was conveyed to the Infirmary, where he soon died. Smith, charged with murder, was found guilty of manslaughter at the Assizes and was transported for seven years.

A jury's recommendation for mercy saved Mark Furniss from the gallows in 1833. A married man, he raped a thirteen year old girl who was searching for lodgings in the town. He was ordered to be transported for life. In 1846 three men received similar sentences for the rape of a twenty year old woman at Ickles, close to the spot where Spence Broughton robbed the King's Mail over half a century earlier. The victim, who was German, lived by busking with her sister in Sheffield and Rotherham public houses. Three other men were imprisoned for conspiring to defeat the prosecution by attempting to send the girl out of the country.

Offences involving firearms were by no means uncommon during this period. Frequently connected with poaching activities, there were also several serious robberies in which guns were used. One such incident occurred at the Surrey Arms, Hollow Meadows, when Joseph Hodkin and Joshua Eastwood, both aged eighteen, burst into the living quarters. Two servants were battered with cudgels and one of the raiders fired a pistol at the landlord, Thomas Greaves. A bullet entered his cheek, lodging in his jaw. It proved impossible to remove by surgery and he was too ill to attend the trial of Hodkin and Eastwood at the Spring Assizes, 1846. The pair admitted they had intended to kill him and rob his house. They were transported for fifteen years. The same year a Handsworth gamekeeper was shot in the face when he confronted a poacher at four o'clock on a May morning, and at Eckington Sir George Sitwell's gamekeeper was severely wounded in similar circumstances. In both cases the assailants were transported for fifteen years.

Transportation was the fate of many convicted of highway robbery, although sentences were hardly consistent. William Bowdler, of whom the *Sheffield Independent* wrote, "a more dirty, ill-looking ruffian was never seen", was transported for ten years for robbing a shoemaker on Derbyshire Lane, after hitting him over the head with a hedge-stake. At his trial in 1840 it was said that Bowdler was a great nuisance in the Charles Street area where he lived, had been several times in the House of Correction, and was believed to be the leader of a gang who had committed many similar robberies in the Heeley and Norton districts.

The robbery of the Broomhill Toll Bar in 1843 resulted in the transportation of Robert Ridge for twenty years, and three accomplices for fifteen years each. Armed with cudgels they attacked the gatekeeper, Pickles Roberts, ransacking his house and stealing £3/5/7d. When arrested all four men were in bed together at a house in Hawley Croft.

Life was the sentence for Samuel Cooper and James Eyre, who robbed a shopkeeper, John Le Tall, in the Park in 1838. Le Tall and his fourteen year old son were pulled from their horse by a band of men as they made their way home to Handsworth. Battered with sticks, they were robbed of twenty-nine pounds in notes, gold and silver.

Coining, passing counterfeit notes, forgery and embezzlement accounted for the enforced emigration of a number of Sheffield people. Henry White, arrested in the Hen and Chickens public house in 1838, with a pocketful of dud shillings, went for fifteen years, despite claiming to be a spy for the Royal Mint. The leader of a gang who passed fake five pound notes in towns throughout Yorkshire was transported for life in 1852, his two accomplices each for fifteen years. A number of Sheffield shopkeepers had been taken in by the notes.

Fraud was considered particularly heinous. John Holmes, who had attempted to pass a forged bill of exchange, was told by the judge who sentenced him to ten years in 1846: "It is a crime that strikes so deeply at the welfare of mercantile men and others who get their living by buying and selling that it must be punished severely." Two years earlier, Sarah Kay, keeper of the Glossop Road Post Office, pleaded guilty at York Assizes to stealing two letters – one containing money and the other a silk handkerchief. The judge, who was reported to have shown "great pain" in sentencing her to fourteen years, said he knew of no offence committed without violence that was more injurious to society than the abstraction of letters from a post office.

Until 1831 sheep stealing carried a mandatory sentence of death. One of the first to be convicted under the amended law was Thomas Gregg, a Sheffield man who had stolen not one sheep, but a whole flock. In sentencing him, the judge at York Assizes said that he should pass the death penalty "to rid the world of one of the greatest reprobates that ever stood at the bar of a court of justice", but that instead he would be transported for life and must be a slave for the rest of his existence. In 1837 two soldiers stationed in Sheffield received similar sentences for stealing two sheep belonging to a butcher. An integral part of the prosecution evidence was that the pair had been seen looking at the sheep the day before they were stolen from a field near to Whitehouse Lane. The following year three Sheffield men were transported for life for killing a lamb at Cooks Wood, near Pitsmoor. The lamb was in a field attached to a slaughter-house and the men cut pieces off it, to eat.

Need to eat was no mitigation in the eyes of the judiciary. Thomas Jackson, who, in 1841, broke into a hen roost at Lightwood, Norton and stole two geese and two goslings, pleaded guilty at Derby Assizes, telling the court that he had been in distress and without food. He was sentenced to fourteen years transportation; the judge told him that he could no longer be permitted to remain in this country as he appeared to be going round purloining anything he could find.

But it was not only judges at the Assizes who ordered transportation. From the magistrates sessions at Sheffield Town Hall many petty offenders were summarily despatched across the seas. The Michaelmas Sessions of 1832, presided over by Lord Wharncliffe, resulted in fifteen transportations. Sheffield was in a severely depressed state, with trade at a standstill and great unemployment, but if the magistrates were aware of the hardships endured by many of those who stood before them – all the offences involved petty thefts – then they were not influenced towards leniency.

Transported for fourteen years were: Matthew Coe, for stealing four ducks in the town; William Walker, a quantity of pigeons; Joseph Bowen, an ass at Dinnington; William Reynolds, stag scales; and George Stephenson, picking a pocket of two sovereigns.

Seven year sentences were passed on: Thomas Barlow and Henry Lark, stealing a coat; Henry Cook, a bag of copper coins; Mary Holgate, a petticoat; James Law, six tame fowls; John Horsman, a quantity of lead; Sarah Greensmith, picking a pocket; George Parkin, entering a house and stealing a hat, coat and pair of boots; John Sadler and Charles Anderton, stealing a gun at Osgathorpe.

During the 1830s and 40s there was growing opposition towards transportation from the Australian colonies. Anti-transportation societies were formed by those concerned that the country was becoming one vast penal colony to which law-abiding people would not wish to emigrate. Demands to stop the shipments of convicts became such that the British government had to look at new methods of punishment. An act of 1853 abolished transportation for anything less than a fourteen year term, providing in its place the sentence of penal servitude.

However, convicts continued to be shipped to Western Australia until 1868. One of the last to be sentenced from Sheffield was George Plant, a brewer's traveller, convicted of stabbing to death William Wilson in Hartshead. Found guilty of manslaughter in circumstances that might easily have led to a murder verdict, Plant was reported to have shown considerable ill-feeling when sentenced to be transported for life.

Many transportees remained in Australia and Tasmania once their terms of punishment had expired. Even those transported for life could obtain a ticket-of-leave after a period of good conduct. The later letters of John Grayson reveal a fairly comfortable lifestyle: he obtained his ticket-of-leave in 1838, and was granted a free pardon in 1846, seventeen years after his arrival in Van Dieman's Land. He married and fathered a family, despite still being legally married to the wife he left in England. Grayson acquired a corn mill in Hobart and prospered for a while before dying in 1850 at the age of forty-seven.

Although a large number of offences carried the death penalty in the early 18th Century, many people who were sentenced to death were not executed. In the years between 1828 and 1834 the death sentence was passed on 8,483 people in England and Wales. Of these, 355 – less than five per cent – were executed, most of the sentences being commuted to transportation for life. One such case from Sheffield in this period concerned Robert Yeardley, aged eighteen, and Luke Sadler, seventeen, who were sentenced to death at York Spring Assizes in 1831 for burning haystacks. Following the intervention of Hugh Parker Esq, who wrote to the judge, stating the concern that was felt throughout the town, their sentences were commuted to transportation for life.

However, between 1800 and 1853 fifteen men and one woman from Sheffield were executed at York. These included a sixty-eight year old man hanged for the rape of a child, and a young mother who killed her seven day old baby by tying a stone round its neck and throwing it into the river at Bridgehouses. Several executions arose out of domestic murders, none more extraordinary in its circumstances than the killing of Mary Nall, by her husband.

Robert Nall stabbed his wife as she lay in bed at a house in Beehive Lane, Glossop Road in 1841. Both were drunk at the time. After realising what he had done he tried to stab himself, then to hang himself, and then he went to Crookes Moor Dam intending to drown himself, but he could not summon the courage to jump in. He returned to the house and allowed his sister to lock him inside while she fetched help. When she returned he had got back into bed and was lying with the body. He was executed on April 9th, 1842.

Charles Turner and James Twibell, both aged nineteen, were hanged in 1830 even though their victim, an overseer at Deep Pit Colliery, survived the savage attack they made upon him. The pitman was knocked down and beaten with a hedge-stake on Manor Lane and lay at death's door for some time. His watch was found in the possession of one of the youths. At their trial a number of witnesses denied their original depositions, a matter which caused the judge great annoyance.

Irrational jealousy on the part of a workmate cause the death of Thomas Froggat. Froggat, a basket-maker, was attacked by Thomas Williams in a workshop at Silver Street Head. Williams had earlier told another man that he intended to "mash Froggat's brains out" as he was trying to steal his quota of work, and without any warning to his victim he hit him across the top of the head with a bill-hook. He was hanged in 1837.

Photos: Sheffield City Council

The two most horrific murders of the period both involved the killing of illegitimate children by their fathers. The first occurred in 1829 when Martin Slack, an eighteen year old brace-bit maker of West Bar, poisoned his small baby with nitric acid. He insisted to the end that the mother, who lived in one room in Norfolk Lane with her parents and six brothers and sisters, had killed the baby. He told the judge who sentenced him to death: "I am not guilty. I am a murdered man, a truly murdered man."

The second – and even more gruesome – case was that of Alfred Waddington in 1852. A twenty-year old razor grinder, living in Lord Street, Park, Waddington was the father of a girl, aged twenty one months, born to a woman who had subsequently discarded him for another man. On a fine August evening he went to the mother's home while she was attending a class at the Mechanics' Institute. An older girl was looking after the child, whom Waddington took from the house, saying they were going for a walk. He went to Cutler Wood at Heeley and killed the little girl by cutting off her head with a shoemaker's knife. He then walked back into town to the Mechanics' Institute, called the mother from her class and told her that the child had fallen off a wall and was injured. The mother rushed with him to the wood, where he attacked her with the knife. She was saved only by her screams, which caused him to run off. The murder aroused great emotion in Sheffield and also at Waddington's trial where Mr. Justice Talford wept openly as he sentenced him to death on December 30th, 1852. He was executed a week later.

Criminal justice in the early 19th Century was both inconsistent and inefficient. Prosecution was a haphazard process, influenced not only by the expense involved, but also by the reluctance of witnesses to wait around the Assizes from the opening day until whenever their case was heard. At that time there was no indication given as to the order in which cases would be brought.

Even in the dock the accused had a very good chance of acquittal. Many charges were dismissed on the most minor of technical errors, quite immaterial to the proceedings. In other cases trial judges inexplicably directed the jury away from a finding of guilt. The trial of George Cutts, from the Park, at York Spring Assizes in 1836 provides an illustration.

Cutts was charged with the manslaughter of Mary Swinden, a woman described in court as "of loose character". They lived together from time to time and one night at one a.m. he went to her house in the heart of the Duke Street slums, broke in and set about beating her with his fists. He dragged her by her hair from an upstairs room, down the stairs and into the outside yard, where he struck her repeatedly with a bedpost. The woman died later the same day. The trial judge, in summing up, emphasised the woman's character, saying she had probably been in many fights. He asked the jury to consider whether she had died from violence unlawfully exercised by Cutts, or from natural causes. They found Cutts not guilty after a few minutes deliberation.

At the same Assizes Robert Ridge was acquitted of feloniously cutting and stabbing an Ecclesfield man, whose arm had required amputating as a result. The judge stopped the case, saying that Ridge had been "labouring under feelings of great anger, due to provocation." Seven years later, when Ridge appeared once again at York, charged with robbing the Broom Hill Toll Bar, he did not receive such judicial consideration. He was transported for 20 years.

The Spring Assizes of 1837 brought more such cases. In one, Joseph Romasarte, a wandering Italian barrel-organist, was acquitted of stabbing a man in the abdomen after a quarrel in the Swan With Two Necks public house. The victim's intestines were left protruding from his stomach but great emphasis was laid in court on the Italian's excitable temperament and the victim's quarrelsome nature.

Even when guilt was proved, violence frequently met with much more leniency than did offences against property. At the 1837 Spring Assizes William Newson, a prisoner in the Debtors' Gaol, was charged with the murder of a seventy year old turnkey, Robert Marshall. Newson had gone berserk in the gaol after being returned there following an escape. He assaulted the turnkey, throwing him against a wall and causing injuries which led to his death ten days later. Found guilty of manslaughter he was sentenced to twelve months hard labour. Had he stolen a sheep or burned a haystack he would, in all probability, have been transported for life.

POLICE: The Early Years

The first inclination towards an organised police force in Sheffield was the appointment in 1818 of Colonel Francis Fenton as Superintendent of Police. Fenton, whose position arose through the Local Improvements Act, headed a small band of men who were, in the main, permanently engaged as constables, rather than appointed annually as in earlier times. In 1825 the force comprised Thomas Flather, John Waterfall, James Wild, William Bland and Thomas Smith. Smith was also keeper of Scotland Street Debtors' Gaol and later kept the Blue Boar public house in West Bar, while remaining a constable.

Colonel Fenton's title was altered from Superintendent to Surveyor in the 1820s. He retired in 1833 at the age of seventy-eight, his efficiency having been seriously impaired for some time. He was succeeded by Thomas Raynor and in 1836 a regular day force was established. Declared by the *Independent* to be "a local improvement, long desirable", it comprised five sergeants and sixteen privates – who doubled as night watchmen. Duty began at noon and ended when the watchmen went out at night. A uniform of blue coats with buttons stamped with the Sheffield coat of arms was provided.

In 1840, in consequence of the Chartist disturbances, the force underwent a considerable increase in strength. In February of that year it was announced that the salary of Thomas Raynor, who had personally arrested Samuel Holberry the previous month, was to be increased from two hundred to three hundred guineas a year. An Act of December 12th "for cleansing, lighting, watching and otherwise improving the town of Sheffield, in the County of York" provided for:

1 Surveyor of Police	@	£3/3/0d per week[1]
1 Inspector	@	£1/10/0d per week
4 Sergeants @ 20s	=	£4/0/0d
22 Policemen @ 18s	=	£19/6/0d
44 Watchmen @ 15s	=	£33/0/0d

Total: 72 men at a cost of £60/19/0d per week.
A special sitting of the magistrates decided that the police district would be an area within a three quarters of a mile radius of the Parish Church.

The incorporation of Sheffield as a borough in 1843 meant the responsibility of maintaining the police force was placed on the Town Council. Control was vested in the Watch Committee and Thomas Raynor became Chief Constable, although he retained the position of Town Surveyor. The force then totalled seventy-five men at a cost of £1,761 for the first half-year and was based at the Town Hall in Castle Street. There was approximately one policeman for every 1,500 inhabitants.

---

[1]Raynor received an allowance for duties as Town Surveyor in his salary of three hundred guineas per year.

By 1852 the strength had increased to 122 men and two years later another fifty men were added. In March 1856 the Chairman of the West Riding Quarter Sessions, Wilson Overend, commenting on a sharp increase in felonies, said "Something must be done – no property is safe under the present state of our protective force." Later that year a further thirty men were added, bringing the total to 202.

In 1858, having reached the age of seventy-one, Thomas Raynor resigned as Chief Constable. In his twenty-five years service he had experienced some turbulent events. Besides the Chartist troubles there had been the 1844 Miners' Strike and the riot at the Medical School, when he had left the premises only seconds before fire broke out. Raynor's successor was John Jackson, who took over on January 1st, 1859 and remained Chief Constable for the next thirty-nine years.

The recruitment of policemen was no easy task, even when other employment was scarce. Rates of pay were lower than those of the average skilled worker and the high risks attached to the job did not make it attractive. In certain areas of the town, notably West Bar and the Crofts, the police were very unpopular with large sections of the public. After one serious stabbing incident in Spring Street, where the assailant, a returned convict, was helped to escape by people who could have apprehended him, the *Independent* commented: "The frequenters of that neighbourhood have too much sympathy with every species of crime and lawlessness and too deep and well-grounded a dislike of the police to take upon themselves the capture of a manslayer."

In such an environment, with violence commonplace, robust police tactics were perhaps to be expected and complaints against officers were frequent, if seldom upheld. In 1834, before the regular force was established, two sergeants of the watch, George Mason and George Crookes, together with two night watchmen, were indicted at the Quarter Sessions for assaulting an epileptic, Thomas Bradwell, in Eyre Lane. Bradwell was knocking on a neighbour's door in mistake for his own when he was seized by the watchmen, beaten up in the street, and then taken to the Town Hall where he was assaulted by all four men. It was alleged that Sgt. Crookes repeatedly twisted Bradwell's nose between his knuckles. The sergeants were acquitted after Thomas Raynor told the court of their good character, while the two watchmen were convicted and fined two pounds each.

The following year Sgt. Crookes was in the dock again after beating a man in the Town Hall, causing severe injuries to his head and legs. He brought as a defence witness Sgt. Mason and was again acquitted after the Chief Constable spoke in his favour.

In 1836 a special meeting of the Police Commissioners was called after two watchmen, Townsend and Barratt, had assaulted a man named John Heaps, putting his life in danger. The same watchmen had locked up another man, refusing to release him until he produced 2/6d. A Select Committee appointed to investigate the incidents expressed great concern as to the manner in which the Watch Department of the police was conducted.

Disciplinary problems pervaded the police force throughout the early decades. Surviving minutes of Watch Committee meetings reveal numerous cases of policemen being fined, reduced in rank and dismissed – in particular for being found drunk on duty.

Drunkenness was one of the social ills of the age. In 1852 there were 1,622 men and women prosecuted in Sheffield for being found drunk (one in every eighty-seven inhabitants) and by the 1860s and 70s the problem within the police force was such that almost every week officers were appearing before the Watch Committee. At one meeting three men, P.C.s Pigott, Dabell and Hueston, were dismissed. At another, P.C. Capps was fined 15/- for fighting in Division Street when off duty and drunk, while P.C. Martin was fined 10/- and reprimanded for creating a disturbance in a pub when in uniform and off duty. Fines or dismissals were ordered for men found asleep on duty, found drunk at home when they should have been on their beats, and found absent from home when on the sick list. Sgt. Matthews, who had been convicted by the magistrates of assaulting a member of the public and fined £3, was merely reprimanded by the Watch Committee. P.C. Chapman, who accused Sgt. Allsop of having spent eighteen months in Derby Gaol, was fined 10/- for being drunk on duty and ordered to apologise to the sergeant in writing.

As early as 1861 the Chief Constable had issued an order forbidding the long-established practice whereby constables escorting prisoners to the House of Correction at Wakefield called at public houses and allowed prisoners who had money to get drunk before being locked up. In 1873, following reports in national newspapers about the conduct of members of the Metropolitan Police, he issued another order stating: "Inspectors should never omit an opportunity of impressing upon their men that it is absolutely necessary to act with moderation and forbearance." However, the number of cases which continued to go before the Watch Committee suggest that his order had little effect upon the men.

The local press were not slow to highlight shortcomings on the part of the police. Following a burglary at Manor Oaks in 1856, where a brewery owner-cum-councillor and his wife were beaten and robbed by armed men, the *Independent* stated: "We have a right to expect that our Watch Committee should maintain such a staff of detectives as to raise to the highest point of probability the chances of detection. A very different course has hitherto been pursued. . . ."

Much criticism was levelled at the methods of investigation employed in the Manor Oaks case. The day after the burglary Inspector Linley visited many houses and haunts of known criminals in the town, arresting three men. They produced alibis and were soon discharged by the magistrates. Eventually Inspector Sills arrested four other men, three of whom were convicted at the Spring Assizes and ordered to be transported for life.

Rivalry between Inspectors Linley and Sills was acute, with both anxious to claim a share of the hundred pound reward offered jointly by the victim of the burglary, William Bradley, and the Sheffield Association for the Prosecution of Felons. Inspector Linley was later alleged by the prosecuting solicitor to have withheld the evidence of a material witness in his eagerness to reap the reward which, in the end, was not paid to either man. There was great argument in the Council Chamber about the way in which the matter had been handled, the Watch Committee concluding that when rewards for the detection of criminals were on offer all organisation disappeared and it was every man for himself.

Inspector Linley found himself out of pocket on the case. He claimed £13/10/8d as expenses incurred in his investigation, but the Watch Committee refused to pay the full amount as he could produce no receipts. They reimbursed Sills his full claim of £4/17/9d, three pounds of which he had borrowed from the Chief Constable in order to pursue the case.

In 1862 Linley was once again at the centre of controversy. He was alleged to have compounded a felony concerning the St. Philip's Cemetery riot, when the sexton, who was prosecuted and imprisoned for disinterring bodies, was later able to claim £200 compensation from county funds in respect of damage to his house caused by the mob. Inspector Linley resigned after twenty-seven years as a policeman.

Despite the malpractice it had been seen to engender, the system of allowing policemen to accept rewards continued. The Watch Committee minutes for November 14th, 1867 show that Detective Officers Jackson and Wheatley were permitted to receive £5/10/0d presented by the victim of a burglary for which four men had been convicted. The following week Wheatley was permitted £1/10/0d for another successful case. In 1868 Detective Officer Carswell was permitted to receive ten pounds for apprehending a man who had escaped from the Sheriff's Officer in London. For some officers rewards were more lucrative than wages of just over a pound a week.

Violence was an accepted part of every day life in Victorian Sheffield. Brawls and affrays, usually precipitated by drink, were a constant problem for the police. Rows among Irish immigrants, who began to settle around Hawley Croft, Solly Street and West Bar in the 1840s, frequently deteriorated into pitched battles among large numbers of people who, on the arrival of the police, forgot their quarrels with each other and turned on the common enemy.

One such incident in July 1855 began when William McCormack attacked John Shannon, a clothes dealer, in West Bar Green, because he would not lend him a shilling. Various relatives and friends joined in what quickly became a fracas and soon afterwards six police officers arrived and seized McCormack. They were dragging him through the streets towards the Town Hall when a crowd, estimated at a thousand strong, closed in on them. In Paradise Square McCormack shouted to his fellow countrymen "Are you going to see me taken?", whereupon an attempt was made to rescue him. In the struggle a stone was thrown, hitting P.C. William Beardshaw, causing injuries from which he later died. James Burke, convicted of manslaughter, was ordered to be transported for fifteen years. McCormack and other rioters who were arrested in their homes the day after the incident were each sentenced to twelve months hard labour.

The following year a battle with pokers, hammers and clubs took place in Hawley Croft between five hundred members and non-members of the Hibernian Society. Many of the combatants were injured and a constable was hit on the head with a brick. He survived, while his assailant, a shoemaker named Patrick Fleming, was fined three pounds by the magistrates for assaulting a police officer.

Unruliness during parliamentary elections was nothing new to the town; the first in 1832 had ended in six deaths when troops turned on rioters. On Election Day 1857 it was the police who faced a mob of around three hundred gathered in Angel Street. Fifty officers guarded the entrance to the Angel Inn where supporters of the Conservative candidate were based. At about four p.m. the officers charged the crowd, who responded by throwing stones and pieces of coal. Several officers were hit, and Edward Prior, a police watchman, received a blow which led to his death eight days later. No-one was charged with causing his death, although Chief Constable Raynor unsuccessfully attempted to prove at the inquest that responsibility lay with a man earlier fined two pounds by the magistrates for throwing stones.

For years to come election days were an excuse for mobs to gather and mayhem to ensue. In 1874, after a meeting in Paradise Square, a crowd, believed to be led by prize fighters imported by the candidates to protect them, ran amok through the town, smashing windows and demanding beer in public houses. Uproar lasted from the afternoon until the following morning. At one thirty a.m. the Ball Inn, Osborne Street, was forcibly taken over by a crowd of four hundred who drew beer at will. Various short sentences of hard labour were later imposed on the small number of participants who were arrested.

Besides the difficulties they experienced maintaining public order, police officers were frequently faced with violent resistance in the apprehension of suspected criminals. A savage attack on two constables, Swift and Howleden, occurred in a field off Shirland Lane in 1863 when they accosted a gang of pigeon thieves. Stealing pigeons from farmers cotes was

---

𝔐agisterial 𝔓roceedings.

SHEFFIELD.

SATURDAY.—Before J. HAYWOOD, Esq., and J. BOWER BROWN, Esq.

A DISORDERLY BEERHOUSE.—Wm. Cliffe, of the Clown and Monkey beerhouse, Paradise square, was summoned on the complaint of Mr. Booth, surgeon, for not maintaining proper order in his house. From the evidence of Mr. Booth and White, one of the detective officers, it appears that the defendant's house is the resort of thieves, dog fighters, and the lowest possible company. In the back part of the premises there was a rat pit, and dogs and rats were kept for the convenience of those of the "fancy" who choose to pay for the amusement. Last Tuesday morning, a large concourse of men assembled at the house to make arrangements for a dog fight. After the fight they again assembled at the house, and there was continued disturbance and quarrels all the afternoon. After one of these quarrels the parties turned out into the Square, where they had a regular pitched battle, each of the combatants having seconders, &c., after the most approved style of "the ring." There were not less than 150 men looking on at the fight, and the disorder may be imagined when it is known that this took place in the middle of the market day, when the Square is occupied with earthenware and other stalls. Mr. Booth produced a memorial signed by every householder in the Square, complaining of the defendant's house as a nuisance. He stated further, that the defendant was in the habit of turning rats loose to breed on his premises, in order to supply his pit. The consequence was that his (Mr. Booth's) cellars were overrun with them....The defendant: Was it likely he should turn them loose when he gave 4s. a dozen for them?....Mr. Haywood convicted in the penalty of 50s. and 8s. costs.

From the 'Sheffield Independent' 1852.

a common activity and the officers noticed that the men's pockets were crammed with birds. One of the gang, armed with a hatchet, chopped off two of P.C. Swift's fingers and dealt him serious blows to the head. P.C. Howleden was slashed in the neck, receiving a cut seven inches long, and

---

a labourer who came to the officers' assistance was hit in the mouth with the hatchet. Two brothers, George and James Law, were later arrested in Birmingham and sentenced to ten years and four years penal servitude for the assaults.

In 1867 P.C. West, while apprehending a barefooted man he saw creeping from a house in the night, was attacked with a poker, suffering serious head injuries, and the following year P.C. Purcell was knocked down and kicked in the neck, causing injury to his jugular vein, while ejecting a troublesome ticket-of-leave man from the Devonshire Arms, Sheffield Moor.

In 1872 P.C. Samuel Gibson died from injuries sustained on duty after being struck on the back of the head with a blunt instrument during a Christmas Day fracas in Spring Street. Gibson and P.C. Pearson were called out to deal with a man named Kennewell, who was assaulting passers-by with a horse whip. While arresting Kennewell, P.C. Gibson was struck by an onlooker. He worked on through the night – without his helmet, which was found on his doorstep the next day with the word 'Death' chalked on it. The seriousness of his injury was not at first realised, but his condition deteriorated in the New Year and he died on February 24th, 1872.

The circumstances in this case highlight the haphazard nature of police investigations in these early days. Before P.C. Gibson died, no arrest had been made in connection with the assault on him, despite a statement from a witness identifying the attacker as twenty year old Samuel Walker, known in the neighbourhood as 'Grinder Joe'. The day after P.C. Gibson's death Walker was arrested, only to be found not guilty by the Assize jury at Leeds.

The trial judge made pointed comment about the delay in arresting the murdered policeman's alleged attacker; about the fact that no deposition was taken from the constable when this was possible; and about the lack of reference to the assault at the hearing against Kennewell, who was sentenced to twelve months imprisonment. P.C. Gibson's widow, who had two young children, received a gratuity of sixty-three pounds from the Watch Committee.

The Penal Servitude Act of 1853, which signalled the beginning of the decline of transportation, introduced a new class of criminal: the ticket-of-leave man.

A prisoner sentenced to penal servitude obtained his ticket after serving approximately half his sentence. Thus many serious criminals who would previously have been transported to the Colonies were now back in circulation after a relatively short time.

The new system was attacked in many quarters. Wilson Overend, Chairman of the West Riding Quarter Sessions, stated in 1856 that, since its

Description of *N°556 Lucy Bernard 3.° Released on Ticket of Leave from Buxton Prison, on the 2nd May 1865.*

Date and Place of Committal	*1 April to Sheffield*
Date and Place of Conviction	*23 May to Sheffield*
Crime	*Stealing an Umbrella*
Sentence	*3 Years P.S*
Trade or Occupation	
Complexion	*Dark*
Hair	*Black*
Eyes	*Dark Brown*
Height	*5 feet 3 inches*
Marks	*An pickled upper front teeth out each teeth decayed*
Period of Sentence Unexpired	*Nil*

Date of each Report.

DATE.	RESIDENCE OF CONVICT.	NAME, TRADE, AND ADDRESS, OF EMPLOYER.
		Committed to the Sessions on a Charge of Stealing a pair of Trousers Goat Nov 24/65

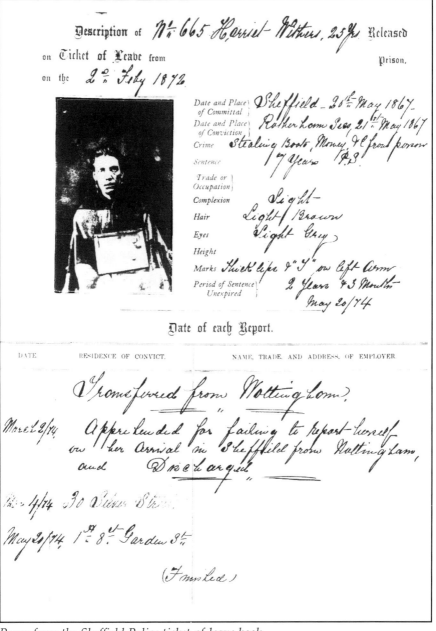

Pages from the Sheffield Police ticket-of-leave book.
Photo: South Yorkshire Police/County Record Office

inauguration three years earlier, there had been 160 committals of ticket-of-leave men in the West Riding for fresh crimes. This was, he maintained, an official exposure of the evils of the system, which involved the prisoner having daily communication with the prison chaplain "whom he endeavours to dupe by flattery, simulation or docility." He believed transportation should be re-introduced and should be for life, saying "it would save the country from a hateful presence which is both a public danger and a moral pest."

In 1863, at the Sheffield Interim Sessions, Overend once again railed against the penal system. Commenting on an increase in the number of cases to be heard, he criticised prisons as being too pleasant and comfortable, adding that a returned convict should be "flogged, flogged and flogged publicly to deter others." With regard to the local situation he said, "There are families in Sheffield, whose names are known, and whose evil propensities to crime descend from father to son and from mother to daughter. Such families ought to be got rid of. They ought never be allowed to remain to increase the criminal classes in this country."

It was certainly true that Sheffield, in common with most large towns, suffered from the presence of returned convicts. The Chief Constable, John Jackson, told the Watch Committee in 1862 that an unusually large number resided in the town. In the previous year thirteen out of fifty-three had been sentenced to fresh terms of penal servitude, leaving forty remaining. Of these he estimated twelve lived entirely by crime, twenty-one sometimes worked but occasionally stole, and seven were obtaining an honest livelihood.

Ticket-of-leave men were blamed for the introduction of what *The Times* described as "a new variety of crime" – garotting. This was a violent form of robbery which involved choking the victim from behind, so as to prevent him or her raising the alarm. The original garotting gangs were said to have learned the technique in the convict hulks. Known as 'putting the hug on', it was employed by guards as a method of convict suppression. Garotting first reached prominence in London in 1856, where it was blamed on the Italians of Whitechapel, although earlier incidents had occurred in Sheffield.

In 1854 a small gang led by William Burkinshaw, aged twenty, committed a series of garotte robberies in the Sheffield Moor area. Burkinshaw was sentenced to death later that year afer a savage assault on a police constable who was escorting him back to Sheffield by train, after he had been arrested in Manchester. The following year William Hague and Richard Hillyard were each sentenced to six years penal servitude for a garotte robbery on a seventy-eight year old man at Grimesthorpe. In typical fashion he was attacked from behind, one seizing his throat while the other emptied his pockets of a watch and 4/6d. During June, 1856 several such incidents occurred. In one, the victim was attacked in his own house in Weigh Lane, Park, when three men stormed in, seized him by the neck and stole twenty pounds and a watch. After these incidents garotting went into decline, both locally and nationally, only to undergo a revival a few years later.

In Sheffield there were several robberies where the victim was lured into a trap by a woman. Henry Kay, a visiting London coal merchant, was walking in Haymarket in 1862 when he was propositioned by a woman. She took him out of the town centre, to Dam Walk, where two men came upon him from behind, one grabbing his throat and pulling him backwards and the other hitting him in the face with a stick. The same ploy was worked on Thomas Sneesby; his attacker was caught and sentenced to seven years penal servitude at York Assizes.

Garotte robberies were a problem for both the public and the police. Many law-abiding citizens, who would not otherwise have considered carrying weapons, armed themselves with knives and other implements in the panic which erupted, especially following the robbery of a man named Burnby in Broomhall Park at Christmas 1864. He was violently assaulted by three men, Dennis Carr and Edward Hall – both of Rockingham Street – and Henry Smith, of Thomas Street. Hall was apprehended only after a fierce struggle with Detective Officer Winn and he received twenty years penal servitude. Carr, the leader of the gang, was sentenced to life, and Smith got five years. A public subscription for the detectives in the case raised £115.

This second wave of garotting provoked loud criticism of the Act of Parliament which had abolished flogging in 1861. Following the robbery of a Member of Parliament on a London street in 1863, however, new legislation – known as the 'Garotters Act' – quickly restored corporal punishment for offences of robbery. The next year the Home Office reduced the periods of remission in penal servitude. A minimum five year sentence was introduced, with maximum remission of one fifth and the first nine months were to be spent in solitary confinement. Sentences of life were to mean that the prisoner was never released. Once again garotting went into decline; this time, apart from the odd, isolated incident, for good.

Feuds and vendettas within the grinders' unions were a major problem for the Sheffield authorities during the mid-century. Incidents of 'rattening' – the removal or destruction of bands which drove grindstones – occurred by the hundred as union members attempted to enforce their rules against those in arrears with subscriptions and against employers who used non-union labour. When rattening failed to have an effect more violent means were introduced. With such actions not officially sanctioned by the unions, and in an atmosphere of intimidation and fear, the police not surprisingly faced great difficulty in apprehending offenders.

The union outrages began to gather momentum in the 1840s. There had been earlier outbreaks – in 1829 two men were transported for life for shooting at a watchman who caught them damaging a wheel in Bower Spring – but the severe depression of 1837-42 brought about a renewed fervour. At York Assizes in 1841 Thomas Booth and John Gregory were convicted of damaging a wheel and grinding stone at Spring Grove Mill, Ecclesfield, and ordered to be transported for seven years, a sentence later commuted to twelve months imprisonment. The following year Abbeydale Works were blown up in a gunpowder explosion which put the owner, John Dyson, out of business. He had employed non-union labour, and three union members who were charged with causing the explosion were acquitted through lack of evidence.

In 1847 there was a temporary crack in the wall of silence after two brothers, Alexander and Thomas Heathcote, were each sentenced to seven years transportation for destroying machinery at Kelham Wheel. The Heathcotes turned Queen's Evidence, stating that the secretary and three members of the razor grinders union had employed them to ratten. The brothers had their transporation orders commuted, while the union men each received seven years.

Gunpowder attacks were not confined to places of work. In April, 1854 the cottages of two scythe makers, at Beauchief and Millhouses, were blown up by home-made bombs. The same week Elijah Parker was shot in the neck as he sat in his cottage at Dore.

The threatening letter was a device frequently employed to intimidate. After an attempt had been made to blow up Messrs. Firth and Sons' Norfolk Works during the Whitsuntide holidays in 1854, one of the partners received the following communication through the post.

Mr. Mark Firth i have to inform you that unless you get shut of those nobstick saw grinders from your weel that we shall Be oblige to try some Remedy of our own. For we now the way into the weel and likewise to the Boiler and allso the warehouse and allso to yourn own Residence and if you think anything about yourself or your Property you will imedetely turn them away or you must Expect wat will follow.

We Remain your
Well Wishers

Only a handful of non-union men were employed by Firths, who offered £50 reward for the capture of the perpetrators of the explosion or the author of the letter. Neither were forthcoming, but several days later one of the saw grinders referred to in the letter had his house destroyed when a bottle of gunpowder was dropped down the chimney.

The first death as a direct result of the union outrages was that of James Linley in 1860. Linley was a scissor grinder who took up saw grinding, which he found more lucrative. He ran his business at the Tower Wheel in Blonk Street, where he kept half a dozen apprentices, who were released at the end of their indentures to make way for new ones. Renowned for his meanness, he was reluctant to pay even the apprentices' pittances. He trained them poorly and, by producing shoddy goods, he was able to undercut union prices.

Several attempts were made on Linley's life. In 1857 he was shot at while sitting in a house in the Nursery[2] and in January, 1859 a can of gunpowder was thrown into a house in the Wicker, where he was staying at the time. In August of the same year he was shot in the head, and died from his injuries five months later. The Coroner's verdict was 'Wilful Murder against some person unknown.'

Acorn Street was the scene of the next fatality. On November 23rd, 1861 a bomb was thrown into the house of George Wastnidge, a fender grinder. There was a great explosion in which Mrs. Wastnidge and a lodger were seriously injured. The lodger, Mrs. O'Rourke, died a few weeks later. A fender grinder, Joseph Thomson, was charged with her murder, but was acquitted at York Assizes. He was, however, expelled from his union.

The blowing up of works and houses and the assaults on non-union grinders, which had continued throughout the 1840s and 50s, showed no sign of relenting even when death had resulted. The week after the Acorn Street explosion a cutler's premises in New George Street, Sheffield Moor, were blown up and in 1862 Joshua Tyzack, who had taken over Abbeydale Works after the explosion of 1842, was shot at five times as he rode in his horse-drawn gig. Tyzack was thought to be in possession of evidence which implicated the secretary of the scythe grinders union in violence against non-union men.

In late 1866 an event occurred which aroused hitherto unseen indignation on the part of the public. In the early morning of October 8th a can of gunpowder was dropped down the cellar grate at the home of Thomas Fearnehough in Hereford Street, causing extensive damage but no injuries. Fearnehough, a saw grinder, was, like James Linley, an employer of non-union labour and had been previously threatened.

Although there had been other more serious incidents, the Hereford Street explosion caught the public's imagination. A subscription fund raised £1,900 to compensate the victim and his family and a further £1,000 was offered as a reward for the discovery of the perpetrators of the explosion. A Committee was formed to take steps to prevent further outrages and this led in May, 1867 to a special Royal Commission to inquire into the Sheffield incidents.

The Commissioners sat at the Town Hall for five weeks, listening to details of 209 cases of violence and twenty major outrages, submitted by the police and interested parties. On the twelfth day, James Hallam, formerly apprenticed to the murdered Linley, broke down and confessed to his part, and that of a man named Samuel Crookes, in the shooting.

---

[2]The area between Bridgehouses and the Wicker, formerly the Duke of Norfolk's Nursery Garden.

William Broadhead. Secretary of the Saw Grinders Union at the time of the 'rattening' outrages. Photo: *Sheffield City Libraries.*

This proved a breakthrough which led to the implication of William Broadhead, secretary of the saw grinders union, as instigator of much of the intimidation and violence over the previous years. No legal action was taken against Broadhead, Hallam or Crookes, or indeed any of the other law breakers who took advantage of an indemnity granted to witnesses judged by the Commissioners to have made full and truthful confessions.

The Royal Commission uncovered the system of intimidation which William Broadhead and others had operated. It did not, however, bring an end to the destructive union feuds, which continued for many years, albeit on a much less violent scale. Rattening went on until well into the 1880s, with about a third of all incidents involving saw grinders. The last reported case in the town was that of John Barrett, imprisoned for two months in 1887.

Social conditions in the lower districts of Sheffield in the second half of the 19th Century were, on the whole, apalling. A report by the Medical Officer of Health in 1873 condemned the regions of courts, terraced and back-to-back houses as promoting disease and crime. The report stated: "Houses and courts exist which are remarkable for their filthiness and for the moral and physical degredation of the denizens." Out of every hundred children born in the town, taken over a three year average, 29·3 per cent died before their first birthday.

Women were systematically ill-treated, many suffering without complaint through fear of further assault or confinement in the workhouse should their husbands be imprisoned. In 1862 there were 240 summonses issued for assaults on women and children; ten years later the figure had risen to 396 and at a Town Council meeting in 1874 it was demanded that magistrates order flogging in such cases.

Lodging houses in the town were particularly iniquitous. Described in the M.O.H. Report as "vile nests of crime, immorality and disease, where thieves, tramps and beggars congregate and migrate, as well as import and transport both moral and physical pestilence", it was suggested that energetic measures be adopted to suppress them.

Immorality in Sheffield had been a topical issue for decades, especially in relation to prostitution. In 1841 a Police Commissioner claimed that morals in Sheffield were lower than in any other town. Prostitution, he said, was a growing evil of amazing magnitude which was sapping the happiness of the community. The following year Chief Constable Raynor estimated there to be 172 prostitutes in the town. Many of these, he said, were girls formerly employed in the manufacturing industries, who had been put out of work by the recession and left without resources.

The Town Hall court reports of the period suggest that a sizeable amount of crime arose out of prostitution. There were numerous robberies and thefts in brothels, though relatively few prosecutions for prostitution – it being necessary to prove that a defendant was 'lewd and disorderly'.

The same week that the Police Commissioners addressed themselves to the problem, the *Sheffield Independent* reported the case of Eliza Johnson, described as "an ill-favoured wench", who was sent to the House of Correction for one month for robbing a man, to whom she had offered her services, of 14/-. On December 17th, 1842 the same newspaper reported "Hannah Terry, a woman fat enough to be the admiration of an African chieftain, and attired in dirty finery, was today charged with robbing William Robinson." She had solicited him in a Waingate public house and taken him to a house in Blind Lane where she "sat in melting tenderness upon his knee." While so doing she stole 12/6d from his waistcoat pocket. The chairman of the bench, sending her to prison for a month, said he hoped it would be of service to her.

The beerhouses of the Crofts district were notorious havens for all manner of low life. John Poole, keeper of one such establishment known as the Snow Lane Tap, was fined five pounds in 1850 for failing to maintain good order in his house. When the police raided it all four beds on the premises were occupied by known prostitutes and men. Poole and his wife were said to have formerly kept a brothel in Hawley Croft.

A case in 1876 attracted great interest in the town when a well known auctioneer named Ball was called as a witness following a police raid on a house in Sands Pavours, Bow Street. In court Sgt. Matthews and P.C. Pinder said their attention had been drawn by seeing "the celebrated Mr. Ball talking to a known strumpet in High Street." They had followed them to the house where they found the auctioneer and the girl in "an indecent position." He suffered acute embarassment and the keepers of the house – a man and woman – were each given a month hard labour.

Two years earlier, on New Years Eve, 1874, there had been excitement in Rockingham Street when no. 129, a notorious brothel, was blown up after a gas leak. The three girls and their customers who were in the house at the time escaped without injury but the proprietor, Mrs. Anne Ashton, was blown into the chimney by the explosion.

Whether or not the Police Commissioner's 1841 assertion on morality in Sheffield was accurate, the extent of prostitution in later years does seem surprising for an inland town with a largely non-transient population. At the time that Thomas Raynor stated there to be 172 prostitutes in the town it was estimated that Hull – a seaport – contained only a hundred. Nor, as the years passed, did the situation in Sheffield improve. The criminal statistics for 1864 show eighty-eight brothels. In 1869 there were ninety-four. Such houses of ill-fame, closely linked as they were with thieving, receiving and villainy of every description, were the citadels of the Sheffield underworld in the mid 19th Century.

By 1865 the police force numbered 241 men at an annual cost of £13,498. Three years later it was increased to 270 and in 1869, through a fear that the Fenian troubles[3] would strike in Sheffield, a further ten men were added.

[3]The Fenians, an Irish revolutionary society, had been responsible for a number of violent incidents in several English towns and cities during the 1860s. However, they did not extend their activities to Sheffield.

William Roebuck, notorious Sheffield 'fence' of the mid-nineteenth century.
Photo: South Yorkshire County Record Office.

But while the police strength increased, so too did crime. Besides the many assaults and rattening incidents involved in the union disputes, the 1860s saw a great upsurge in the number of burglaries committed in the town. Private houses, public houses, factories, shops, warehouses and pawnbrokers were regular targets, and in 1867 even the YMCA fell victim.

Although the 1864 criminal statistics show thirty receiving houses in the town, the prosecution of receivers was quite rare. Much excitement was generated in September, 1862 when a High Street jeweller's shop was raided by police and twenty-eight gold watches which had been stolen in a Swansea burglary five years earlier were found. The jeweller, Benjamin Cohen, was charged and released on a thousand pounds bail but committed suicide before he could be tried.

Another notorious local fence – who was brought to justice – was William Roebuck, known among his peers as 'Stretcher'. For twenty years, from 1845, he dealt in watches and jewellery, bought fron thieves in Sheffield and towns all over the North. His speciality was 'putting off' stolen watches – re-setting one watch in another case so as to make it difficult to identify. His skill was such that he defrauded many pawnbrokers by passing off gilt and base metal as pure gold and he was said to keep a huge nugget of gold, melted down from watch cases, at his home in Rockingham Lane. When he was arrested there in 1865 and charged with being concerned in a burglary at a Hull jeweller's, police found hundreds of pawn tickets relating to jewellery he had pledged for cash. The *Sheffield Independent* commented: "The prisoner has often eluded the grasp of justice but on this occasion it is almost certain that he will be fairly laid by the heels." Roebuck was sentenced to ten years penal servitude at Leeds Assizes in March, 1865.

William Roebuck was a professional criminal who lived by the proceeds of larceny. Such a man was undoubtedly dishonest in the extreme – but the most notorious villain of the century was yet to come.

CHARLIE PEACE: A Man of Aliases

In the annals of British criminal history there are few more colourful characters than Charles Frederick Peace. Ruthless killer, skilful burglar, master of disguise, animal lover, musician, braggart, hypocrite and womanizer – Peace lived a full life in his forty six-years, despite spending almost a third of it behind bars. Tales and myths about his crimes, his escapes and his many other extraordinary deeds are legion. His life story, not least as portrayed in newspapers, novels and films, is pure folk legend.

Charlie Peace was born on May 14th, 1832 in a little house in Angel Court, which lay at the corner of Nursery Street and Lady's Bridge, Sheffield, the youngest of three surviving children. His father had been a collier in Burton-on-Trent before joining a travelling show as a trainer of wild animals. After arriving in Sheffield he had worked as a shoemaker, but shortly after Peace was born the family moved to Stanley Street, off the Wicker, where the father took up business as a coal dealer and carter.

Pitsmoor School and Hebblethwaite's School in Paradise Square provided the young Peace with his education. Methodist meetings, which he attended with his father, instilled in him religious knowledge which would surface sporadically throughout his life. At the age of twelve he began an apprenticeship as a tinsmith, but soon went to work in the rolling mills.

On the morning of his fourteenth birthday Peace was working at Millsands Rolling Mills when a piece of red-hot steel pierced the back of his left leg, emerging just below the front of the knee. He was operated upon, without anaesthetic, at the Infirmary, where he remained for the next eighteen months, when he was discharged as incurable. Peace overcame the injury, learning to walk so as to disguise it, and became a man of great agility, not least in his burgling activities.

His life of crime began in his early teens when he took up the art of picking pockets, a speciality being the shammed collapse, which led to any person who was kind enough to help him to his feet being relieved of their valuables. He frequented the roughest public houses, where he became acquainted with thieves and prostitutes, besides entertaining on the violin. He had taken lessons on the instrument from a watchmaker, Joe Bethley, who lived in Division Street.

Peace's first conviction was in 1851, at the age of nineteen. Together with a man named Campbell he broke into Mount View, the home of Mrs. Catherine Ward, and stole a quantity of jewellery and two pistols. It is an indication of the times that a respectable elderly lady kept guns in the house. Peace sold one of the pistols to a man named John Ward – an alias he would use himself in later life – who lodged with his mother in Scotland Street. The other was pawned at a shop in the Park and traced back to Peace, who was sent to the House of Correction for a month, while his accomplice was acquitted.

Photo: South Yorkshire Police.

After his release from prison Peace returned to Sheffield and his life of pub musician and house burglar. He became proficient as a 'portico thief', or cat burglar, entering houses through upstairs windows, via the stone canopies over the front doors. It was by this method in 1854 that he burgled the house of Mr. H. Hoole J.P., at Crookesmoor, and other residences at Brincliffe Edge and Nether Edge, stealing jewellery and, from one house, seven pairs of boots. Peace's sister and another woman were arrested while attempting to pawn one of the pairs of boots in West Bar. His mother's house in Bailey Field was searched and a large quantity of stolen goods found. It was back to the House of Correction for Peace, now twenty-two, this time for four years penal servitude.

While serving this sentence Peace made an escape bid which failed and, seemingly in frustration, attempted to commit suicide by slashing his throat with a nail he had somehow acquired. He was not granted his ticket-of-leave and served the full sentence, being released in 1858.

Now a fully confirmed criminal, Peace began to spread his wings, travelling from town to town, staying a few weeks before moving on. In 1858 he met Hannah Ward, a widow with a six month old son, Willie, and took her as his wife. Shortly afterwards he was arrested in Manchester, together with Alfred Newton, keeper of a beer house in Spring Street.

The pair had burgled a large house and had left the loot hidden in a sewer to be collected later. When they returned the police were waiting and after a fierce struggle both men were arrested. Peace gave his name as 'George Parker', describing himself as a professor of music who lived in Nottingham. He called his mother as a witness to say that he had been at home all the week in which the burglary had been committed. It was to no avail: he was sentenced to six years penal servitude while Newton got eighteen months.

Peace served his time in various prisons, including Millbank, Portland and Chatham, where he was involved in a mutiny which resulted in him being flogged and transferred to a convict settlement at Gibraltar. In 1864 he was granted his ticket-of-leave and returned to Sheffield to his wife, stepson and young daughter, Jane, who had been born two months after he went to prison. He started a picture framing business from their home in Kenyon Alley (between Edward Street and Upper Allen Street) and later took a shop in West Street.

It seems that during this period Peace may have tried to live an honest life but fate decreed it was not to last. He became seriously ill with rheumatic fever and his business collapsed. By the Summer of 1866 he was back at his old game and in August he was arrested again, while burgling a house in Manchester.

On this occasion Peace, usually careful not to combine drink and work, rendered himself incapable on the householder's whisky and was no match for the servants of the house who were disturbed by his noise. Charged under the name 'George Parker, alias Alexander Mann' he made a

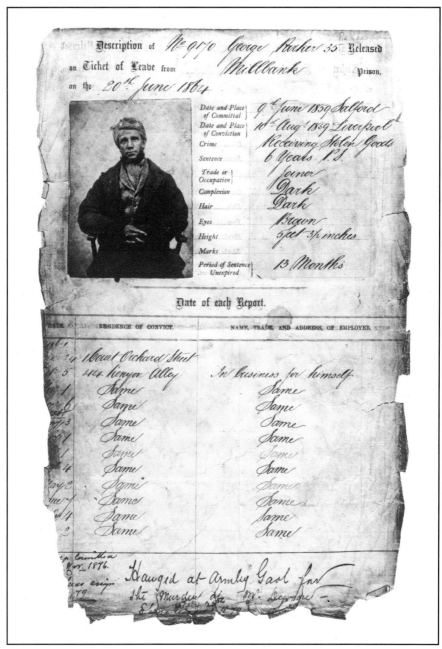

Photo: South Yorkshire Police.

pathetic, grovelling plea to the judge to give him mercy, not for himself, he said, but for his children. It was to little effect; the judge referred to his previous conviction in 1859 and said if he had been truly penitent he would not have committed the latest offence. He sentenced him to seven years penal servitude – it was to be the last prison sentence Peace would serve.

He was released in 1872 and returned to live in Orchard Street. A short time later the family moved to Scotland Street, before going out of town to Darnall in the Spring of 1875.

At Darnall, then a village, Peace moved into a small, terraced house – number 40, Victoria Place, Brittania Road. Next door-but-one, number 36, was occupied by Mr. and Mrs. Arthur Dyson, who had recently returned to Sheffield from America, where Dyson had been a railway engineer. Peace was attracted to Katherine Dyson and set out to woo her, initially via her young son, to whom he demonstrated his trained parrots and pigeons. The Dysons, however, soon became irritated by their neighbour, who imposed himself upon them, and Mrs. Dyson, with whom Peace later claimed emphatically to have had an affair, began to reject his advances.

Peace was not a man to be easily rebuffed. He screamed insults at husband and wife in the street, tried to trip up Mr. Dyson – who was six feet six inches tall – as he walked along the pavement and on one occasion, with three neighbours present, pointed a revolver at Mrs. Dyson's head, threatening, "I'll blow your bloody brains out and your bloody husband's too."

Eventually the Dysons could stand it no longer and moved to the other side of town, to a small terraced cottage below the Banner Cross Hotel on Ecclesall Road. Their relief at having got away from Peace, however, soon suffered a setback when he appeared at their new home on the very day they moved in. He told them that he was there to annoy them and gave vent to a series of obscenities and oaths. Having destroyed their peace of mind he then disappeared for a month.

On November 29th, 1876 Charles Peace paid a visit to the Vicar of Ecclesall, the Reverend Newman, to discuss his new parishioners, the Dysons. He claimed the couple were wicked and that Mrs. Dyson had ruined his business. After subjecting the vicar to a long tirade, during which he offered to show him proof of his affair with Mrs. Dyson, he left the vicarage and prowled about Banner Cross Terrace, outside the Dyson's home. He told a passer-by, Mrs. Sarah Colgreaves, that Mrs. Dyson was his "bloody whore" and to a labourer he said, "I'll make it warm for them before morning. I'll shoot 'em both."

At eight p.m. the Dyson's next door neighbour, Mrs. Mary Ann Gregory, saw Mrs. Dyson pass the back window and shortly afterwards heard her scream. Arthur Dyson rushed from his cottage, turned into the passage at the side of the terrace, and Peace, who had caused Mrs. Dyson to scream, pulled the trigger of his pistol. The first bullet missed, hitting the wall. Peace fired again, this time striking Dyson in the left temple. He died at 10.45 p.m. in the home he had occupied for only a month.

On December 5th, 1876 an inquest was held at the Stag Inn, Psalter Lane, into the circumstances surrounding Arthur Dyson's death. The Coroner's jury had no hesitation in finding a verdict of wilful murder against Charles Peace. Later that month a reward of £100 was offered out of government funds to anyone offering evidence that would lead to his discovery and conviction. It is interesting that, after controversies over rewards in earlier years, the notice specifically excluded 'any person employed in a police office' from making a claim.[1]

Having shot Dyson, Peace headed for his mother's house in Orchard Street, via the Broomhill Tavern, where he caught a cab for town. His wife and family had moved to Hull in July and he made his way there, but took lodgings away from them in another part of the town. He stayed in Hull a few weeks before taking off on a burgling spree all over the country, staying at Bristol, Bath, Birmingham and Nottingham, where, in lodgings kept by a receiver of stolen goods, he met another woman who would have a profound effect upon his fate. Susan Bailey, thirty-five and separated from her husband, was not initially attracted towards the elderly-looking Peace but she soon succumbed to his attentions and they set up home together in Nottingham as 'Mr. and Mrs. John Thompson'.

All the while Peace was burgling regularly and successfully. On one occasion, so he later claimed, he returned to Sheffield and walked past Inspector Bradbury – the man in charge of the Banner Cross murder case – before burgling a house in Havelock Square. From Nottingham he and Mrs. Bailey moved back to Hull, taking lodgings in the home of a police sergeant. He briefly renewed contact with his wife, who believed he was simply on the run and had no idea of his relationship with 'Mrs. Thompson'. While staying with the police sergeant, who thought Peace was a travelling dealer, he committed many burglaries, frequently taking the loot back to his lodgings.

Peace had several narrow escapes. In Hull he avoided arrest only by shooting at a pursuing policeman and, having moved back to Nottingham, he and his mistress were disturbed in bed when the house was raided. Peace told the police his name was 'John Ward' (his mother's old lodger) and, after persuading them to leave the room while he got dressed, escaped out of the window and across rooftops.

Eventually the pair arrived in London, living at several addresses until, having done some very profitable burglaries, Peace took up the lease on a large house in Peckham. He sent for his wife, Hannah, and stepson, Willie,

---

[1]Although payment of rewards to police officers for the arrest of criminals was not officially abolished until 1924.

to join him and his mistress, attended the local church, and presented himself to all around as a paragon of respectability with 'private means'. He was aware of the reward for his capture and had taken steps to disguise his appearance by shaving off his hair at the front and staining his face brown with walnut juice. The fact that he was much sought after did not deter him from burglary and, with the aid of a horse and gig, he was active by night all over London.

Early in the morning of October 10th, 1878 Peace left a house in Blackheath via the drawing room windows and found officers of the Metropolitan Police waiting for him. He fired five shots from his revolver but one officer, P.C. Edward Robinson, grappled with him, despite being shot through the arm, and wrestled him to the ground. Arrested, Peace gave his name as 'John Ward' and his age as sixty. At the Old Bailey on November 19th he was convicted of attempted murder of the policeman and was ordered to be kept in penal servitude for the rest of his natural life.

In Newgate Prison Peace's complexion began to lighten as the dark brown of the walnut juice faded. His real identity was already being questioned when he wrote a pathetic letter to a former neighbour in Peckham, requesting that he visit him, signing the letter 'John Ward'. The curious neighbour went to Newgate and was greatly surprised to find that 'John Ward' was none other than his old neighbour 'John Thompson'. He immediately went to the police who visited the 'Thompson' household at 5, East Terrace, Peckham and found an abundance of stolen property and an arsenal of burglar's tools and firearms. Peace's wife, stepson and mistress had fled.

Susan Bailey, or 'Mrs. Thompson', was soon found, however, and, after checking with the police that the £100 reward was still on offer, confirmed the true identity of Peace as well as helping to trace his wife, who was arrested at the home of her daugther and son-in-law in Hazel Road, Darnall. Mrs. Peace was later prosecuted at the Old Bailey for receiving stolen goods but was acquitted, it being considered that she had been acting under the instruction of her husband.

Peace's days were now numbered. His prospects suffered a severe blow when Mrs. Katherine Dyson, who had emigrated to America following the murder of her husband, was traced and returned to Sheffield, eager to give evidence against her former neighbour. Already sentenced to live out his life in prison, Peace now found his life itself in jeopardy.

On January 17th, 1879 he was brought from London by train to face the first hearing of the murder charge against him, before the Sheffield Stipendiary Magistrate, Mr. E. M. E. Welby. Peace was represented by Mr. – later Sir – William Clegg and the witnesses who gave evidence, besides Mrs. Dyson, included various people Peace had spoken to at Banner Cross on the night of the murder.

Throughout the proceedings he frequently interrupted. He complained that he could not hear witnesses, objected that a man sitting in court was sketching him – the man was actually a newspaper reporter, taking notes – and declared to one witness, "Oh you villain. God reward you!"

He told the Stipendiary, who admonished him for interrupting: "I beg you pardon, sir, but my life is at stake and I am going to vindicate my character as well as I can. If you don't want me to speak, put a gag in my mouth." Later he accused the prosecuting solicitor of putting words into a witness's mouth, adding that he had seen a great deal of injustice done in different courts but he was not going to have any done in that one. "I am not a dog," he said. "My life is at stake. If you hang me it will only free me from a long, dreary life of penal servitude, and I don't care much which way it is; but I am going to have full justice done me."

At the end of the day the case had to be adjourned until the following week and Peace was remanded to Pentonville Prison. A huge crowd had assembled outside the court and the warders had great difficulty in pushing through to their transport. At the railway station police and porters had to form a tunnel for the prisoner and his escort to reach the train, such was the throng.

The following week, while travelling back to Sheffield for the adjourned hearing, Peace made a daring bid to escape. With the train travelling at 50 m.p.h., and handcuffed to a warder, he threw himself through the train window. The force of his totally unexpected movement dragged the handcuffs off the warder, and Peace fell to the ground, dazed and bleeding. He was still there when the warders, having halted the train, ran back along the track. He later claimed that he had intended to kill himself.

Several thousand people awaited the party's arrival in Sheffield. Peace was taken to the police station in Water Lane and given medical attention. The adjourned hearing, held in the candle-lit corridor outside his cell, was marked by his groans, complaints and requests for a surgeon. Eventually he was committed for trial at Leeds Assizes, whereupon he asked the Stipendiary: "Will you let me sit before the fire a bit before I go? I'm really very badly." His request was turned down.

Peace was tried at Leeds Town Hall on February 4th, 1879. He pleaded not guilty to the charge of murder but there were none of the scenes of earlier hearings. The *Sheffield Daily Telegraph* described him as "a shabby, wretched-looking old man, looking as if all hope had left him; grey hair closely cropped; cheeks hollow; lips pale; but the eyes steely keen and restlessly watchful."

He was represented by Mr. Frank Lockwood, later to become Recorder of Sheffield and Solicitor-General. Peace's only line of defence was his claim that he had shot Dyson accidentally, while struggling, after the latter had taken hold of him. His counsel battled away relentlessly in cross-examining Mrs. Dyson – the only witness present when the shots were fired – to get her to admit a struggle, but she never wavered. Nor could she be trapped into admitting the intimate relationship with Peace which he had claimed; letters allegedly written by her to him were produced as evidence but she denied all knowledge of them. She did agree that she had been to a music hall with Peace on one occasion, and had also been with him to Sheffield Fair, where they had their photograph taken together. While this may have fuelled speculation as to the actual relationship they had enjoyed, it did nothing to help Peace's case.

The jury took only ten minutes to find him guilty of murder and he stood quite still as Mr. Justice Lopes donned the black cap and passed sentence of death. As he left the court Peace remarked to his escort: "I am going to hang for something I done but never intended."

In Armley Prison Peace was closely guarded night and day, following a letter to the Director of Convict Prisons from the Director of Great Scotland Yard. The letter stated:

'I have the honour to acquaint you that information has been received by the police that efforts will be made by the relatives and friends of the convict Peace to prevent his being executed, should he be found guilty of murder, by conveying poison to him in order that he may commit suicide. It is stated that the convict has previously made arrangements with his friends that, if at any time he should be condemned to death, they were to visit him and carry with them in their mouths poison wrapped in tinfoil which was to be passed to him in the act of kissing.'

It later transpired that this story had emanated from Peace's former mistress, Mrs. Susan Bailey, alias 'Mrs. Thompson'.

In the death cell Peace spent much of his time reading religious works. A week before his execution he asked if he could see the Vicar of Darnall, the Reverend J. H. Littlewood, whom he had first met in the Wakefield House of Correction, when the latter was a prison chaplain. Their paths had subsequently crossed when Peace and his family moved to Darnall and, when not plundering the larger houses of the North, Peace had been a regular attender at the Reverend's church, where he taught at the Sunday school. The vicar travelled to Leeds and Peace told him he had nothing to gain and nothing to lose in his present position as he knew he was going to be hanged and would rather end his days than face the prospect of spending the rest of his life in penal servitude. He then went on to confess to a second murder, that of Police Constable Nicholas Cock in Manchester in 1876, for which a young Irishman, Aaron Habron, was sentenced to death but later reprieved to serve penal servitude for life.

Peace said that he had been burgling a house in Manchester when he was confronted by the policeman. He had fired to frighten him but the bullet had struck the young officer in the chest, causing fatal injuries. Peace

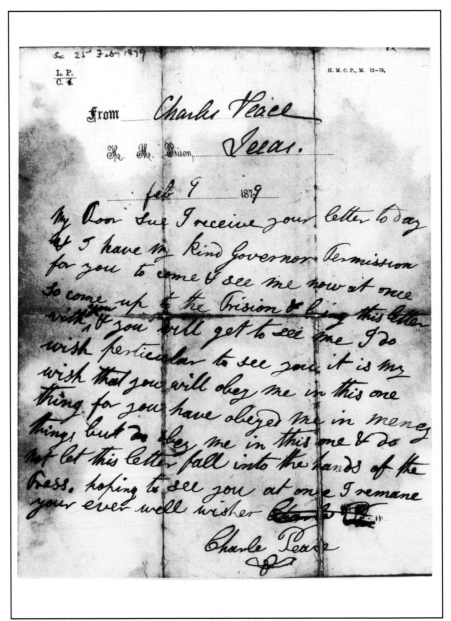

Charlie Peace; letter from the condemned cell to his former lover Mrs. Susan Bailey,
written shortly before his execution.
Photo: South Yorkshire Police.

had escaped and Habron, who sometime earlier had had a disagreement with P.C. Cock and had threatened to kill him, was arrested and convicted at Manchester Assizes. The trial had taken place on November 27th and 28th, 1876 and Peace had observed the whole proceedings from the public gallery. The day after Habron was sentenced to death he had returned to Sheffield and shot Arthur Dyson. Some months after Peace's execution the innocent Habron, who had protested vehemently and repeatedly over the two-and-a-half years he had spent in prison, was released with a free pardon and £800 compensation.

Peace spent his last days writing letters which exuded Christian sentiments. His wife, stepson and daughter all visited him and found him in good spirits. His former mistress, Susan Bailey, travelled to Leeds in the hope of seeing him but was refused entry to the prison. Shortly afterwards she wrote to the Home Secretary claiming the hundred pounds reward for his conviction.

On the day of execution, February 25th, 1879, Peace went to the scaffold, erected in the prison courtyard, without protest or struggle. A large crowd had gathered outside the prison throughout the previous night and Peace's last words, addressed to a group of newspaper reporters who were present to witness the event, could be heard clearly over the prison wall. He stated that his last respects were to his wife and children. As the hangman was adjusting the rope to his neck he asked for a drink, but it was too late. The rope was fitted, the lever pressed and his villainous life was ended.

It is ironic that the act which led Charlie Peace to the gallows did not involve burglary or theft. In his life of crime he had, by his own admission, used a gun on many occasions to resist arrest, but the Banner Cross murder arose simply out of his rage at being spurned by a woman.

As a professional criminal Peace might appear a failure if one considers the amount of his life spent in prison. On the other hand, between his release in 1872 and his arrest at Blackheath in 1878 he was at his most active and successful, despite being sought by police forces all over the country during the last two years. By then he had learned the lessons of his youth and always worked alone, visiting in advance houses he intended to burgle, and working out the easiest methods of entry and getaway. He always maintained a respectable appearance, wearing decent clothes and carrying his tools in a violin case or travelling bag, and he employed his capacity for disguise to the full.

In wealthy areas Peace would often burgle half a dozen houses, one after the other, in a night and he was not averse to returning on a later occasion to take what he had been unable to carry the first time. In 1877 he twice burgled the home of Lord Shaftsbury at Wandsworth, each time stealing large quantities of jewels. Diamonds were his speciality, along with gold and silver plate, which he carried in a large pocket sewn inside his coat.

Possibly the last photograph of Charlie Peace, taken after his final arrest (at the time he was still known to the police as "John Ward").

As to where Peace disposed of the goods he stole, that mystery has never been solved. In his last few years he committed hundreds of burglaries but the loot found in his London home and that of his daughter in Hazel Road, Sheffield was clearly only a very small proportion. One theory is that he fenced it abroad, for in 1876, while still living at Darnall, Mrs. Dyson received three letters from him, all postmarked in Hamburg, Germany. Whatever the truth, it remained Charlie Peace's secret to the end.

KILLERS, CONMEN & OTHERS

During the years between the executions of Alfred Waddington in 1852 and Charles Peace in 1879 there were few murder cases in Sheffield, despite the high level of violence to be found in parts of the town. Such killings as did occur resulted in manslaughter verdicts and sentences of penal servitude. In only one case was the death sentence carried out in the period – that of Joseph Myers, a Hoyle Street saw grinder who murdered his wife in 1864. Myers tried to cut his own throat but was taken to the Infirmary, where he recovered. He was later prevented from committing suicide a second time, only to be hanged at Leeds.

The 1880s brought a sharp upsurge in local murder with three men hanged during the decade for domestic killings. In the most gruesome, in 1884, Joseph Laycock cut the throats of his wife and four small children at their one-up, one-down home in White Croft. Laycock, a part-time militia man, was notorious in the neighbourhood for his drunkenness and violence. He had been out of prison less than a week when he murdered his family.

A number of domestic incidents came perilously close to murder. In 1887 Walter Townsend, a nineteen year old file grinder, shot his young wife three times in the face as they walked on Mushroom Lane. She had nagged him about his low wages. Townsend went to prison for five years. In 1891 Isabella Edge, a teacher at Darnall Board School, was horribly disfigured after being shot, also in the face, by William Hall, whose offer of engagement she had turned down. Hall was sentenced to fifteen years penal servitude. At this time revolvers could be bought easily for a few shillings.

The murder of Sarah McConnell at Christmas 1905 inspired the *Sheffield Independent* to report: "The annals of crime might be searched in vain for a murder so revolting as that for which Harry Walters, a Sheffield miner, was yesterday sentenced to death at Leeds Assizes. Compared to it the horrors of the Jack the Ripper tragedies pale almost into insignificance. . . ." The murdered woman had been found with multiple stab wounds in her home, a squalid court in Allen Street. Walters, her cohabitee, maintained that when he had found her naked body she was already dead, but despite conflicting evidence and the judge summing up heavily in his favour he was convicted of murder and executed.

However, the murder trial of the period was that of Miss Felicia Dorothea Kate Dover, accused in February, 1882 of poisoning her employer, Thomas Skinner. The courtroom at Leeds Assizes was packed with spectators, Victorian fascination for murder never being stronger than in cases where the defendant was an attractive young woman.

The victim, Skinner, was a widower who lived in Glover Road, Heeley. In 1880 Kate Dover went to work for him as his housekeeper, but she soon set her sights on becoming his wife. She was very jealous of her predecessor, a Mrs. Jones, with whom Skinner was still on friendly terms and in December, 1881 his former housekeeper gave Skinner a chicken. Before cooking it Kate Dover went out and bought an ounce of arsenic, which she put into the stuffing. During the meal Skinner became violently ill and later died.

Initially Dover denied all knowledge of how the arsenic came to be in the stuffing. She admitted buying it but maintained that Skinner, an amateur artist, had asked her to do so as he wanted to colour some artificial flowers. She then changed her story, saying that she bought the arsenic to improve her own complexion. In the dock she admitted poisoning Skinner, but claimed that she intended only to make him ill, hoping that he would blame Mrs. Jones, who had given him the chicken.

The press dubbed Kate Dover 'The Queen of Heeley'. She appeared in the dock wearing a fur jacket and dark gown, a straw hat trimmed with black lace, kid gloves and a veil. She was found guilty of manslaughter by the jury, and it was only the skill of Frank Lockwood, defending, that saved her from a verdict of murder and the death penalty. When Mr. Justice Cave sentenced her to penal servitude for life she fainted and had to be carried from the court. The 'Queen of Heeley' was removed to Armley Gaol and later to Pentonville, never to be heard of in Sheffield again.

Street violence showed no signs of relenting as the nineteenth century gave way to the present one. Disturbances and affrays were commonplace, especially after the pubs had closed, and weapons were used indiscriminately. One of the toughest parts of the town was the Scotland Street area, heavily populated with Italian immigrants.

Most of the male Sheffield Italians worked as street musicians or ice cream vendors. Arguments among themselves, in which the police were none too eager to get involved, often ended in bloodshed. At one Saturday night party in 1898 Luis Raffo was seriously injured by blows to the head with a hatchet. His assailant was discharged at the Quarter Sessions. Vincenzo Biancucci, who had changed his name to Vincent White, was sentenced to four years penal servitude and ordered to be then deported for stabbing his Irish wife, almost severing her hand. Giovanni Colorossi, an organ grinder, was deported in 1892 for a murder committed in Italy before he had emigrated. His identity came to light after he stabbed a Sheffield man.

With the notion of 'going quietly' still alien to the nature of many criminals, police officers frequently found themselves involved in desperate struggles when making arrests. At Meersbrook in 1884 P.C. George Vardy was stabbed by a man whom he had arrested and handcuffed. The man, George Gregory, somehow managed to withdraw a knife from his clothing and inflicted a wound two inches deep in P.C. Vardy's neck. The officer struggled with him for half an hour and was on the verge of collapse through loss of blood when assistance arrived. Gregory was given twenty-one months hard labour for inflicting grievous bodily harm.

Five years later, in Harvest Lane, P.C. Prior was stabbed in the face and hands by two burglars whom he had caught in the act. At their trial one was sentenced to eight years penal servitude, despite tearfully begging the judge for mercy. The injured constable was awarded two pounds for his bravery, Mr. Justice Manistry suggesting that he should not look at the monetary value of the award, rather the feeling the judge had on the matter.

With guns readily available it was not only the criminal classes who posed a danger to the policeman on his beat. In 1898, while examining the rear of premises in West Bar, P.C. Thomas Kelly was shot in the face by the occupier of the property, an auctioneer, who mistook him for a burglar. The man was charged with unlawful wounding but acquitted at the Quarter Sessions.

Perhaps surprisingly, sentences in manslaughter and serious wounding cases of a century ago appear to have been often quite lenient. When, in 1888, the Recorder, Frank Lockwood Q.C., passed sentences of two months and one month imprisonment on two men who had brutally assaulted a Snig Hill chemist, there was anger in many quarters and protest meetings were held for several weeks. Among letters to the *Sheffield Daily Telegraph*, one, signed 'Justice Dethroned' suggested that "Five years and the cat would have done something towards putting a stop to these outrages." In 1898 the stabbing of a woman in the throat – in view of two policemen – warranted six months imprisonment, while a year earlier a collier, Thomas Simmons, was given five months hard labour for the manslaughter of a man on a tram. The victim had assaulted a woman in the dram shop of the Lady's Bridge Hotel and Simmons had followed him on to the tram, seized him by the throat and struck his head several times, after which he returned to the dram shop and had a drink. There were a number of sentences of three and six months for manslaughter and non-fatal stabbings in the 1880s and some even lighter, like William Proctor who got fourteen days for killing a man with a file during a quarrel.

Conversely, burglars tended to receive heavy sentences, reflecting the judiciary's traditional priority for property over person. Long periods of penal servitude were common. The Prevention of Crime Act 1909 introduced an even stiffer penalty, Preventive Detention[1], and at the October Quarter Sessions the following year the first case in Sheffield was heard under the new legislation. James Higgins, aged forty-six, pleaded guilty to burglary 'whilst he was leading a persistently dishonest and criminal life'. The Recorder, Mr. J. Scott-Fox K.C., was told by Detective Inspector Ibbotson that Higgins had led a criminal life for twenty years and kept the company only of convicted thieves. He was sentenced to three years penal servitude, to be followed by five years preventive detention – a total of eight years imprisonment.

---

[1] A persistent offender, i.e. one with several previous convictions for similar offences to that which they were charged, could be sentenced to a period of imprisonment additional to the sentence for the current offence.

Juvenile burglars could expect to be sent to a reformatory or to be flogged. Seventy-one of those who appeared in Sheffield Children's Court between January and October, 1909 were ordered to be flogged, so many that Mr. J. Pointer, M.P. for Attercliffe, drew the Home Secretary's attention to the numbers and asked in the Commons whether he would consider the advisability of forbidding such practices with legislation. The Home Secretary replied that he was quite satisfied with the way justice in Sheffield was administered.

The late 19th and early 20th Centuries brought some colourful conmen and fraudsters to Sheffield. Baron Fritz von Weisenberg, who claimed to be a nephew of Prince Bismarck, a cousin of Count Waldeck and a relative of the Duke of Albany, cut a flamboyant figure around Walkley in the 1880s. Married to a local woman, he had a manservant, travelled by pony and trap, and indulged in high living to an extravagant degree, all obtained on credit. His role as a wealthy member of the landed German nobility came to an abrupt end when he was arrested at his home in Highton Street. Various people in different parts of the country had been fooled by his claims, in particular a German baker in London who had 'loaned' him £650. At the Old Bailey the 'baron' was sentenced to five years penal servitude.

Another conman to collect five years was 'Lieutenant Charles Douglas of the Royal Navy'. Known also by at least four aliases, Douglas dressed in full officer's uniform, including double-breasted frock coat, claiming to be an inspector of recruiting officers for the Royal Marines. His trail of trickery, which principally involved running up bills in hotels and public houses, came to a close when he was arrested by Detective Inspector Thompson of Sheffield Police in 1885. He had enjoyed the hospitality of officers at Hillsborough Barracks for several days and was planning to hold a dance in the town.

James Henry Irving Cruickshank, who described himself as 'Captain', gave his address as the Wharncliffe Hotel, Sheffield when arrested on a charge of defrauding Lady Randolph Churchill in 1897. He had persuaded her to 'invest' £1,550 in a railway syndicate. Tempted by the attraction of quick and substantial profits she had succumbed to his glib talk, as had many other society ladies whom he had conned over a long period. Cruickshank was sentenced to eight years at the Old Bailey.

'Baron' von Weisenberg, 'Lieutenant' Douglas and 'Captain' Cruickshank were travelling confidence tricksters who were coincidentally based in Sheffield at the time of their arrest. Albert Marson, however, celebrated in his day as the 'Pitsmoor Millionaire', was a local deceiver. At his trial in 1902 at Leeds Assizes it took prosecuting counsel four hours to outline the case against him, such were the complexities of his devious activities.

Marson obtained money by representing that he was heir to a vast estate in Canada, rich in gold and minerals. On the basis of this claim he 'borrowed' three thousand pounds from Thomas Eastwood, a cycle manufacturer, who believed he was investing money to be used in extracting the minerals. In 1899 an article appeared in the magazine, *Pearson's Weekly*, describing Marson, then aged twenty-nine, as "the coming richest man in the world. "At the time he was employed in an iron works at 30/- a week.

It is a reflection either of Marson's ability as a conman, or – more likely – his victim's gullibility, that the two of them discussed the article in the 'Millionaire's' cramped little house in Bramber Street, where Eastwood agreed to part with more money. Marson told him that he would receive five thousand pounds for every pound 'invested' and, attempting to impress Eastwood further, began signing letters to him: "Albert, the future Lord Syerston." Eventually, if rather belatedly, the cycle manufacturer became suspicious and Marson was arrested. Instead of mining for minerals in Canada he ended by breaking rocks in Portland Gaol. Long forgotten now, the 'Pitsmoor Millionaire' was a household name in Sheffield in the early years of this century and must rank as one of the more bizarre characters in the city's criminal history.

The police force, which numbered 177 men when John Jackson became Chief Constable in 1859, had increased to 470 by the time of his death in 1898. Jackson, still working at the age of seventy-seven, was a popular Chief. His successor, Commander Charles Scott, an ex-Indian Army man, took up his duties in November, 1898.

Commander Scott's fourteen years in office coincided with a relatively uneventful period from a criminal point of view. However, a unique incident of public disorder occurred due to the activities of the suffragette movement, whose campaign was gaining momentum throughout the country at this time. In 1909, at Edmund Road Drill Hall, a crowd estimated at between eight and ten thousand women gathered and tried to force their way into the hall, where the Prime Minister, Herbert Asquith, was addressing a meeting. Numerous scuffles and fights broke out between suffragettes and the police, and many constables received scratched and swollen faces. The *Independent*, reporting "some vigorous bouts of fisticuffs" in a piece headed "MOB LAW – POLICE AND PETTICOATS!", declared: "Nothing could have been more praiseworthy than the way in which the force restrained themselves, and suffered indignities which would have justified them in taking very severe measures." While the suffragettes' struggle continued for many years to come there were no recurrences in Sheffield of the Edmund Road fracas.

Drinking within the police force was a seemingly intractable problem which Scott had inherited from his predecessor. Even the Watch Committee disagreed among themselves as to how culprits should be dealt with; at a Committee meeting in 1894 one councillor expressed regret that some of his colleagues were all too eager to unjustly criticize the police. At that meeting a constable was spared dismissal by seven votes to six. But while the drink problem had never put John Jackson's position in jeopardy, it proved too much for Commander Scott.

In September, 1912 a scandal erupted in the city following the discovery of a number of police officers in the Police Club on a Sunday. This was in defiance of an order from the Chief Constable, prohibiting the opening of the club on Sundays. Three of the best known senior officers in Sheffield, Chief Inspector Speechley and Inspectors Andrews and Cotterill, were all alleged to have been found drunk in the club. The Watch Committee instituted an immediate inquiry.

An offer of indemnity was made to any police officer giving information of other irregularities of which the Watch Committee were unacquainted. This caused much controversy and ill-feeling and was withdrawn after several days, but in the meantime the Committee had received sufficient information to incriminate Chief Inspector Speechley, who, after twenty three years service was reduced to the rank of constable, while Andrews and Cotterill were absolved.

The root of the trouble was said to be the practice of senior officers drinking with subordinates, something considered not conducive to good order and discipline. In a sensational climax to the inquiry Commander Scott resigned. When he died in 1926 The *Sheffield Mail* wrote: "The internal troubles of the Sheffield Police Force weighed on him heavily during his last days here."

Shortly after Major John Hall-Dalwood arrived as Chief Constable in 1913 the First World War broke out. Almost immediately the city's crime rate dropped. "Crime in Sheffield has been practically infinitesimal," said the Recorder, Mr. John Scott-Fox K.C., in his opening address at the October Quarter Sessions in 1914. Only nineteen people faced charges, compared to seventy-three for the same period in the previous year. Commenting on this, and on Sheffield's contribution to the war effort, the Recorder declared that the reputation of the city was preserved, maintained and strengthened. He went on the deal with the few cases of shop burglary and petty theft which was to be a typical sample of crime for the rest of the war.

The most serious offences of the war period were those which contravened the Defence of the Realm Act. Patriotism was such that when Albert Bright, an iron merchant, was sentenced to penal servitude for life in 1916, for obtaining undisclosed information from a munitions worker at Messrs. Vickers Ltd, there was a widespread feeling that he had been very fortunate to be spared the death penalty. The charge against Bright was that he had obtained the information from 1905 onwards – long before the war was anticipated – and that he had uttered the words, "Us Prussians have as much right to live as anyone else." Mystery surrounded the case since Bright was not Prussian, nor could it be established what he intended to do with the information. There was no evidence that he had communicated it to a third party.

Injudicious talk led to the prosecution of sixty-seven year old William Evers of Ecclesfield the following year. He had offended passengers in a railway carriage at Midland Station by announcing that "The war will never be over as long as people give their money. There are three of the rottenest men in the Government as ever lived." Evers told the court he was very anxious about the huge expenditure on the war. He was fortunate to escape with a five pound fine.

Hoarding food led to a fine of £100 on John Albert Hill in 1918. When his business premises in Bernard Road were raided there was found 5,200 lbs of tea (rations for 1,500 people for a year), 830 lbs of flour and cereals and 290 lbs of jam, soup, bottled fish and meat. Hill's explanation was that he had two servants at his home in Hastings Road, Millhouses, and as he was going away on business he considered it necessary to leave ample provisions for them! The hoard was ordered to be confiscated.

In one of the more illogical and misplaced displays of anti-enemy feeling, in 1915, a large crowd of people attacked the Attercliffe premises of shopkeepers whose German ancestry suddenly caught up with them because of the war. Tills were rifled and stock looted as the crowd, many of them wives of soldiers serving abroad, ran rampage. Among the 'alien' victims were one man who had been born at Wadsley Bridge, another born in Attercliffe of German parents, and another born in Grantham of naturalized parents. Fifty-three of the rioters later appeared in the Police Court.

More confusing were the origins of Max Emmanuel Hohenwarth. When arrested while working on munitions at Tinsley, Hohenwarth was wearing the DSO, the French Legion of Honour and the military decorations of several other European countries. He had been in Britain since 1884 and had been conscripted into the British Army in 1916, leaving in circumstances which were not made public, shortly before his arrest. He first claimed to be British and then Swiss, but the magistrates decided he was probably German – and dangerous – and should be interned.

With the war over and life returned to normal, the Sheffield public's interest in murder was reawakened when, on September 16th, 1922, police officers discovered the body of a Chinese man, trussed up in a trunk and buried in the cellar of his Crookes laundry.

Sing Lee, aged thirty-three, had owned the laundry at 231, Crookes, where he also lived, for several years. A popular man in the neighbourhood, he employed two assistants – a fellow countryman, Lee Doon, and a local girl, Lily Siddall. Sing Lee was last seen alive on the evening of Saturday, September 9th, 1922, when he asked Miss Siddall to work as

Sing Lee: Murdered at his Crookes laundry in 1922.
Photo: Sheffield Mail.

usual on the following morning. When she arrived on the Sunday there was no sign of Sing Lee, and when she asked Lee Doon where the boss was he said, "Gone to China", adding that he, Lee Doon, was now in charge of the business.

Lily Siddall's curiosity was aroused on the Monday when she saw two men digging a hole in the cellar floor, and on the following day when she found Lee Doon wearing Sing Lee's trousers and noticed the latter's trilby hat hung up. She asked Doon why the boss had not taken his hat and he replied that he had gone to town on the Saturday night and bought a new one. Becoming very suspicious by now, because Sing Lee could not have had time to go to town as she had not left the laundry until 9 p.m. on the Saturday, Lily Siddall travelled to Liverpool, where she knew Sing Lee had relatives. They returned to Sheffield with her and the odd circumstances were reported to the police, who visited the laundry.

The body of Sing Lee, a man five feet four inches tall and of muscular build, was found under a pile of coke in the laundry cellar, in a trunk measuring 2ft. by 1½ft. by 1ft. 10inches. Also in the trunk were items of blood-stained bedding. Lee had gaping wounds to his head, extensive fractures to the skull, and a rope fastened tightly round his neck. A police surgeon concluded that he had been attacked while in his bed, and other blood stains were found in the room in which he slept, above the laundry.

No. 231, Crookes. Scene of the Chinese laundry murder.
Photo: Sheffield Mail.

Lee Doon was at the laundry when police arrived. Asked where his boss was he replied "gone", and when shown the body he said, "me no understand." A hammer and hatchet were found in the kitchen. Doon was arrested and subsequently committed for trial.

At Leeds Assizes, Lee Doon, whose command of English was very poor, was represented via an interpreter. He claimed that he and Sing Lee had quarrelled about the laundry owner's habit of smoking opium, that Lee had insulted him and had challenged him to fight. As they fought Sing Lee had fallen, hitting his head on the stove. When he realised Sing Lee was dead he panicked and put the body into the trunk. He then paid two unemployed labourers £1 each to dig the hole in the cellar floor, into which he placed the trunk.

Lee Doon's explanation was at considerable variance with the prosecution evidence, particularly that of the police surgeon. No evidence of opium smoking was found at the laundry and it seemed quite clear that Lee Doon's motive for killing his employer had been one of robbery. He had a large amount of money in his possession when arrested, including two banknotes believed to have been paid to the laundryman shortly before his death.

Doon was convicted of murder and sentenced to death. In the death cell he asked several times if he could be beheaded, instead of hanged, in accordance with his native custom. Utterly calm and dispassionate from the moment of his arrest and throughout his trial, he remained so until the end. He was hanged at Armley Prison on January 5th, 1923.

The Crookes laundry murder attracted nationwide interest. At the inquest on Sing Lee, press men from all over the country crammed into Sheffield mortuary, and the trial of Lee Doon was reported in great detail. Had it not been for the vigilance of Lee's young employee, Lily Siddall, the killer may not have been arrested, for it was known that the dead man was planning to return to China for a holiday, and Doon's explanation for his disappearance was in some part plausible. Likewise, given time, Lee Doon might have chosen to leave the city, or indeed the country, and the murder, described by the *Independent* as "one of the most sensational crimes Sheffield police have ever investigated", might never have been solved.

GANGMEN AND GAMBLERS

In his first annual report as Chief Constable, in 1914, Major Hall-Dalwood raised the matter of the "infection of the betting spirit" which pervaded Sheffield. Concerned about the obsessive enthusiasm with which large numbers of the population indulged in the illegal backing of horses, he expressed the opinion that betting was the cause of twenty-five per cent of poverty among the working classes.

In the East End and the Park betting was rife and had been for years. The growth in literacy since the introduction of state education meant that racing information was readily available via the newspapers and bookmakers no longer needed to travel to race meetings to find customers. Instead they haunted the gates of such works as Firths, Jessops and Edgar Allens, while their touts on the inside collected bets among the workforce.

The opportunity to accumulate a few shillings or pounds for a modest outlay was a temptation to which many eagerly succumbed. A survey conducted in four large works in 1913 estimated that out of six hundred men in various departments, 486 were habitual backers. It was, said the Reverend Benson Perkins (who launched an anti-gambling crusade after spending two years in the East End), a moral disease which affected even young boys, who could be seen in the streets of Attercliffe betting on whether the next tram to pass by would be an odd or even number.

Increased wages through munitions work served only to exacerbate the situation during and immediately after the First World War. In 1923 one local street bookmaker stated that he regularly made £100 per day and said he knew of many others who made similar sums. A policeman, one of twelve on regular duty to watch for street betting, said that, although only forty-six bookmakers appeared in the census for Sheffield, he believed there to be nearer a thousand.

Gambling was not restricted to horse racing. On Sunday afternoons betting men gathered at several locations around the city to play cards, dice, and pitch and toss – a simple game in which three coins are tossed into the air and bets are made on the proportion of heads or tails which will show as they fall to the ground. It was said that on any fine Sunday afternoon in Dunlop Street, Attercliffe at least thirty separate groups of men and youths could be seen playing pitch and toss, while a police raid on Tinsley Park Wood – known locally as 'Monte Carlo' – in 1911 surprised a crowd of over a hundred, all but one of whom escaped. The man who was caught was fined 25/- for illegal gambling and assaulting a police sergeant.

The most organised, and most lucrative, tossing ring was held at Sky Edge, a high ridge of wasteland overlooking the Park district slums. Started before the First World War by a group of local bookmakers and racing men, it attracted hundreds of gamblers daily, some from as far away as Rotherham, Barnsley and Chesterfield. Betting went on from mid-morning until dusk, the organisers collecting a toll on all bets made in the ring. Its elevated position meant early warning could be given if the police approached, although several spectacular raids were made during the war, when large numbers of deserters were rounded up.

By 1919 the tossing ring at Sky Edge was under the control of a band of men whose name was to become infamous in Sheffield criminal history: the Mooney Gang. Originating in West Bar, they had a reputation for violence and thieving and, when not engaged in nefarious activities on Northern racecourses, had intimidated licensees and law-abiding citizens in the rougher parts of Sheffield for almost a decade. Led by George Mooney, then aged twenty-nine, many of the gang had grown up together from early childhood. Closely allied with the Mooneys were a group of men from the Park, chief of whom was Sam Garvin, a thirty-nine year old local villain with a criminal record dating back to 1904.

For a while all was well, with the tossing ring providing plenty of cash for its organisers. But the wartime boom did not last and by the early 1920s the steel industry slumped and wages dropped accordingly. By the beginning of 1923 there was no longer sufficient cash to satisfy all those involved and George Mooney decided to dispense with the Park men in order to provide a greater share-out for himself and his immediate henchmen.

The outcome of this decision was the formation of a rival force: the Park Brigade. Headed by Sam Garvin, the new gang soon had dozens of recruits and, heavily outnumbered, it was the Mooneys who were driven from Sky Edge. Not surprisingly there was anger and bitterness on their part and very soon their thoughts turned to revenge.

In the small hours of Sunday, April 23rd, 1923 William Furniss was dragged from his bed in a Duke Street Lane tenement and beaten unconscious by two men wielding pokers. Furniss, aged thirty-two, was a prominent member of the newly formed Park Brigade and the assault marked the outbreak of a gang war which was to continue in Sheffield for the next five years. The assault on Furniss was avenged a month later by the razor slashing of one of his attackers, Frank Kidnew. Kidnew received a hundred cuts to his body.

On June 16th the Park Brigade stormed George Mooney's home in Corporation Street and tried to smash their way in, only to be met by a hail of bullets. A Park man, George 'Ganner' Wheywell, was hit in the shoulder and, when police entered the barricaded house, they found the principals of the Mooney Gang in possession of a double barrelled shotgun, a rifle, revolver and ammunition. Mooney was later fined ten pounds for possessing the firearms, but denied shooting Wheywell, claiming that he had been injured by his own friends.

Throughout 1923 the assaults and skirmishes continued, the Park Brigade pursuing the Mooney Gang, which soon fell apart, the members fighting among themselves as well as with their common foe. Several incidents resulted in short sentences of imprisonment, but most of the cases which went to court were dealt with by small fines.

On Christmas Eve 1923 the Park Brigade staged their heaviest attack on the Mooney's home. Armed with razors, Sam Garvin and three others smashed their way in and terrorized Mooney and his family. One of the raiders told his fifteen year old daughter: "We've come to wish your father a merry Christmas." This proved the last straw for Mooney, who escaped serious injury only by hiding in an upstairs cupboard. Shortly afterwards he left Sheffield and did not return for another year.

Having eliminated all threats to their exclusive control of the Sky Edge tossing ring, the Park Brigade did not let up in 1924. On December 8th they gathered in Fitzalan Square and paraded to Furnace Hill, where lived Tommy Rippon, a former Mooney cohort. A bullet and bricks through the window signalled their arrival and they proceeded to smash up the house and assault a visiting friend of Rippon's with stool legs. Five Park Brigade members were arrested; when asked what had started the trouble one replied, "Old broth being warmed up."

Early the following year the Mooney Gang underwent a brief revival – without its former leader – culminating in an attack on a Park man outside the Edmund Road Drill Hall. The man's life was in danger for ten days after he was hit on the head with an iron bar. When his assailant appeared in court it was stated by the prosecution that witnesses had expressed their fear of giving evidence against him. Intimidation of witnesses was a regular feature of gang trials – many prosecutions failed as a result – but on this occasion the defendant was convicted and given eighteen months hard labour.

A turning point in the gang feuds came with the murder of William Francis Plommer on April 27th, 1925. Plommer, a labourer and father of four children, had neither criminal convictions nor connections with gangs. He was fatally stabbed outside his home in Princess Street, Norfolk Bridge, because he had insisted on seeing fair play the previous evening during a fight between two men, one of whom, Wilfred Fowler, was a follower of Sam Garvin.

On the night of the murder Garvin and a group of men, including Wilfred Fowler, combed the neighbourhood of Princess Street, asking the whereabouts of Plommer's home and making threats to kill him. Plommer, unarmed, approached six of the men and offered to fight them one by one. He was knocked down and stabbed in the stomach by a sharp instrument, while on the ground. He died in his home shortly afterwards. The murder weapon was never found.

Shortly before the assault on Plommer, Sam Garvin and three others left Norfolk Bridge by tram. Alighting in the Wicker they rushed up to a man named Harry Rippon outside the Bull and Oak public house and struck him with a razor and cosh. For Garvin, who had done more than most to incite the others to assault the luckless Plommer, it was to prove a timely alibi to a murder charge.

On July 28th ten Sheffield men were charged at Leeds Assizes with the murder of William Plommer. At the end of the trial, which lasted four days and involved eighty witnesses travelling daily from Sheffield, two brothers, Wilfred and Lawrence Fowler, were found guilty of murder and sentenced to death. Three men were convicted of manslaughter: Amos Stewart and George Wills, who were each sentenced to ten years penal servitude, and Stanley Harker, sentenced to seven years. Five men, including Sam Garvin, were acquitted.

Wilfred Fowler was twenty-three years old, his brother Lawrence was twenty five. They were convicted on the evidence of a handful of witnesses who spoke of having seen one or both of them with a short bayonet or dagger. Strenuous appeals were made on their behalf in an attempt to have the death sentences commuted, but to no avail. Lord Chief Justice Swift considered that they had been rightly convicted and the Home Secretary, in a letter to the Fowlers' solicitor, stated that he failed to see any grounds which would justify him advising a reprieve.

The Fowlers were hanged at Armley Prison, Wilfred on September 3rd and Lawrence on the following day. On the eve of his execution Wilfred was said to have made a full confession, exonerating his brother from all blame. The Home Secretary later denied the existence of such a statement, but Lawrence Fowler maintained his innocence to the very end. The execution of the Fowler brothers was an emotive and controversial issue in Sheffield for years to come, many people believing that others were equally, if not more, guilty of Plommer's murder.

The day after he was acquitted of being involved in the Princess Street murder, Sam Garvin appeared again in the dock at Leeds Assizes. He was charged with wounding Harry Rippon in the Wicker on the night Plommer died. True to character he denied all knowledge of the assault, despite the evidence of a number of independent witnesses who said they had seen him slash Rippon on the head. Convicted by the jury, he was described by Detective Sergeant Flint of Sheffield Police as a very dangerous man, one of the cleverest criminals in Sheffield. After telling Garvin it was his duty to pass a very substantial sentence, the judge, Mr. Justice Finlay, gave him twenty-one months hard labour.

Garvin's acquittal on the murder charge did not, it seems, meet with the approval of George Mooney. The day that the Park man was sentenced to twenty-one months Mooney was returning by train from a race meeting when a fellow passenger addressed him on the subject of his arch-enemy. Mooney attacked the man, breaking three of his ribs and biting off part of his ear. He went to prison for nine months hard labour as a result.

On May 1st, 1925 a small squad of hand-picked police officers was formed in Sheffield and given the express task of suppressing the gangs. Following the Plommer murder four days earlier, the Chief Constable had received instructions from the Home Office that urgent measures must be taken. The founder members of the squad, Sgt. William Robinson and P.C.s Walter Loxley, Herbert Lunn and Jack Farrily, were transferred to plainclothes duty and given a free hand to pursue their objective. They quickly became known as the Flying Squad.

The Flying Squad carried the war into the enemy's camp, frequently ejecting gangmen from pubs where they were having a quiet drink and roughing them up outside. Their methods were controversial, somewhat dubious from a legal viewpoint, but successful. After one celebrated incident P.C.s Loxley, Lunn and Farrily were all summonsed for assault by George 'Ganner' Wheywell. The police alleged Wheywell had struck Lunn after refusing to leave the Red House, Solly Street, but Mr. Harry Morris, for the battered gangman, suggested to the constable: "What Wheywell has done to you, you paid back at four thousand per cent interest!" The outcome was three months hard labour for Wheywell, with the charges against the Flying Squad dismissed. In another case where Mr. Morris represented a man charged with assaulting P.C. Loxley, the defendant appeared in court swathed in bandages. The solicitor, drawing the magistrates' attention to his condition, which the police said had arisen through him falling down some steps, suggested that he should be charged, not with assault, but with attempted suicide.

Frequently outnumbered in dangerous situations, the Flying Squad fought gun, razor and cosh with fist, boot and truncheon. Rather than wait for trouble to arise they went looking for it – and the gangs soon got the message. Many years later, looking back on his time as leader of the squad, William Robinson said: "We kept after them all the time. We harried them until we wore them down."

During the autumn of 1925 rumours began to circulate that all was not well within the Sheffield Police Force. The position of the Chief Constable, Hall-Dalwood, became a subject for speculation when, after a meeting of the Watch Committee in October, it was announced that he had been granted a month's leave of absence on account of ill-health.

Hall-Dalwood never returned to his duties and resigned on January 7th, 1926. At a presentation to him by members of the Force, in March, he made a speech which caused astonishment in Sheffield. He spoke of "evil attempts" to undermine his authority and "insidious influences from outside" which had worked against him, saying that his position had at times been intolerable.

Although he received demands from many quarters to elaborate, Hall-Dalwood made no further public comment. During his twelve years in charge he had repeatedly urged the Watch Committee to strengthen the force, but neither the reasons for his resignation, nor the nature of the "insidious influences" were ever revealed.

The next Chief Constable, Captain Percy Sillitoe, made a great impact upon the people of Sheffield during his five years in the city. An outgoing man who clearly revelled in publicity, he took up his duties on April 1st, 1926, the first day of the General Strike. At that point Sam Garvin, George Mooney, and several other principal gang men were in prison and the gangs were, in the later words of P.C. Walter Loxley, "bent, if not broken". Sillitoe capitalized on this state of affairs and, with the aid of some astute appearances in the Police Court, where he addressed the magistrates on the gang problem, plus judicious comments to the press, his fame soon spread far beyond Sheffield. The *Pictorial Weekly*, applauding his work during his first year, described Sillitoe as "the doyen of England's higher police officers."

Folklore, assisted by his own memoirs, *Cloak without dagger*, credited Sillitoe with being 'The Gang Buster'. Hall-Dalwood's contribution went without recognition. There is no doubt that much of the work had already been done before Sillitoe arrived, but he certainly consolidated that work, increasing the strength of the Flying Squad and supporting his men to the hilt. The squad was finally disbanded in 1928, the gangs having been finally crushed and the Sky Edge tossing ring driven out of viable existence by repeated police raids.

On their release from prison, both George Mooney and Sam Garvin returned to Sheffield. Mooney, after a 1927 tangle with the Flying Squad which resulted in a battering and a two month prison sentence, retired from gang affairs once and for all and lived out the rest of his life as a law-abiding citizen. Garvin, while occasionally standing as a bookmaker on the Northern courses, continued his life of villainy, adding to his already extensive criminal record until he died in the early 1950s.

Just as the latter days of Commander Scott and Lieut.-Col. Hall-Dalwood had been darkened by internal police problems, so Capt. Sillitoe did not escape what must have begun to seem like a curse on Chief Constables of Sheffield.

Throughout the tossing ring boom, street betting had continued unabated, many bookmakers operating almost under the noses of the police. An explanation as to how this had been possible – at least in one area of the city – became clear in January, 1930, when three police constables and nine bookmakers stood together in the dock at Sheffield Police Court, charged with offences of bribery.

In the preliminary proceedings it transpired that a number of police officers from Brightside Division – a figure of twenty was mentioned – had consistently accepted small amounts of cash from bookmakers between 1922 and 1929. In return the bookmakers had been allowed to run their businesses without disruption. The only time the system lapsed was for a twelve month spell during 1925 and 26 when one plain-clothes officer refused to accept cash; the rest of the time all went smoothly. Whenever an officer left, his successor was introduced to the bookmakers. The system came to light after a new Superintendent was appointed to Brightside in 1929.

All officers suspected of having an involvement were interviewed by the Chief Constable. It was alleged that some were given the option of admitting that they had taken bribes and giving evidence against the bookmakers, or alternatively standing alongside them in the dock. To the three policemen who were prosecuted, an inspector involved in the investigation was said to have commented: "I am sorry for you men, because for every £1 you have had other men have had £20."

However, after preliminary proceedings which lasted nine days, two of the accused officers were discharged by the magistrates on account of lack of evidence, leaving only P.C. Joseph Moxon to stand trial with the bookmakers at Leeds Assizes.

In April, 1930 P.C. Moxon was found not guilty, while three of the bookmakers were convicted of bribing a number of policemen, eleven of whom appeared as prosecution witnesses and openly admitted accepting money. The man considered to be at the centre of the system of corruption, William Aistrop, was fined £250, the judge sparing him imprisonment after the jury had stated their belief that he had been under pressure from the police to bribe them. Aistrop, aged forty-eight, who described himself as a grocer, was regarded as the most prosperous bookmaker in Sheffield, with a turnover of thousands of pounds a week. He conducted his business on Brightside Lane, on a stretch between the Blucher and the River Don public houses. He had been convicted of betting only three times in the previous five years.

Frank Pacey, who was fined fifty pounds, with fifty pounds costs, had taken bets on the same spot in Popple Street for six-and-a-half years without once being convicted. When, in 1924, he was told by a policeman that, due to the large number of complaints about betting in the street an arrest would have to be made to satisfy senior officers, Pacey simply arranged for one of his 'runners' to be arrested.

The third bookmaker, George Parkin, was also fined fifty pounds with costs. He was convicted on thirty-two counts. He was told by the judge: "I do not believe that there is any evidence that you ever really pressed a man to accept a bribe who was not ready and willing to accept it."

In his summing up Mr. Justice Humphreys severely critized Brightside Division, saying that the situation which had operated for years had been most lamentable. "Part of the force has been shown in this court to be rotten to the core," he said, adding that it was very painful for citizens, used to looking up to the police force as men who could be trusted, to find eleven men from the same division giving evidence that they received regular bribes as a price for failing to do their duty. Referring to the police witnesses who had repeatedly denied involvement, until it became clear that unless they made admissions they would be prosecuted, he said, "It has been shown as clearly as can be shown that the effect on the mind of a police officer of accepting small sums of money is that, in many cases, he becomes an inveterate liar, a person who is utterly useless as a police officer, because if you cannot believe a police officer you might as well get rid of the police force. The whole of the confidence the public has placed in this particular division of the Sheffield force has been misplaced."

At the conclusion of the case the prosecuting counsel, Mr. C. Paley Scott, made a statement to the court. He said there was a danger that, unless the real circumstances were understood, the general public might think that the Sheffield police had been sheltering themselves behind the prosecutions of bookmakers. He added that, after consultations with the Director of Public Prosecutions and the Attorney-General, it was felt that there was insufficient evidence against the constables, leaving no other option but to prosecute the bookmakers. Mr. Justice Humphreys replied that he had no doubt the Chief Constable would make every effort to clear the slur which had been cast upon the city police force.

Capt. Sillitoe made no public comment about the Brightside scandal, but was said to be privately disgusted by the conduct of the officers involved. At a subsequent meeting of the Watch Committee fifteen police officers were dismissed from the force and another seven fined for dereliction of duty. The following year Sillitoe left to become Chief Constable of Glasgow. He went from there to Kent and ended his career as Director General of MI5. He died in 1962. Although it is over half a century since he left Sheffield, Sillitoe's name is still held in the greatest esteem by many older citizens and ex-police officers who remember his time in office.

BLACKOUT AND BLACK MARKET

By comparison with the preceding decade, the 1930s were uneventful in terms of crime in Sheffield. Between 1928-32 indictable offences reported to the police fluctuated around three and a half thousand annually, but in the next five years there was a decrease, until in 1938 the figure had fallen to 2,792.

The police force, headed by Major F. S. James, who succeeded Captain Sillitoe, had an establishment strength of 708 by 1935. In that year the detection rate for crimes reported was 69.16 per cent, a figure which has never since been equalled.

One problem which had not receded was illegal gambling. As war loomed and munitions work alleviated the large scale unemployment of earlier years, the police made their presence felt among the betting fraternity. In 1937, in the West Bar, Attercliffe and Hammerton Road Divisions, there were combined totals of 224 prosecutions for street betting and thirty-seven in respect of houses used for betting purposes. The new affluence was reflected in prosecutions for drunkenness, which rose from 156 in 1932 to 519 in 1939.

Coincidental to the outbreak of war, the city's crime statistics reached a record 4,407 in 1939, a twenty-seven per cent increase on the previous year. This was reflected mainly in offences against property, in particular burglaries on houses, shops and warehouses, with the total value of property stolen in the year £15,817. The era of bank hold-up, payroll snatch and large scale safe robbery, in which sums far in excess of this annual figure would be stolen at a stroke, lay in the future. In the meantime criminal activity was focussed on the unique opportunities presented by the effects of the war.

In the wealth of material that has been written about Sheffield during the Second World War, little mention has been made of wartime crime. One may speculate on the reasons for this, but perhaps the anti-social and predatory aspects of profiteering and looting have been deemed best forgotten by those responsible for nostalgic accounts of a community pulling together through difficult times.

But crime there was. While there are no official statistics, nor Chief Constables' Reports, for the years 1941 to 1944, the war, not least through rationing and the black market, introduced many otherwise law abiding and honest people into the – albeit small-time – world of crime. Reporting in 1946, at a time when many of the wartime restrictions were still in force, the Chief Constable stated: "It must be borne in mind that the cumulative effect of rationing and shortages has created a ready market for practically any kind of goods. One of the major difficulties of the criminal in normal times is the disposal of stolen goods, but today a substantial portion of the population – even persons who would normally be appalled at the idea of being involved in a criminal transaction – are only too ready to accept goods at extortionate prices without any question as to the source of supply."

However, it was the blackout, not the black market, which occupied the attention of the authorities during the early days of the war. Breaches of regulations prohibiting the display of lights during the hours of darkness met with stringent fines and in some cases imprisonment. In October, 1939 a Spital Hill man who had left on a bedroom light which could be seen from outside during the blackout was sentenced to two months at the Police Court. The same month the *Star* reported: "There has been a perceptible decrease in crime in Sheffield since war broke out. One of the reasons advanced for this is that people have too much else to do and to think about."

A contradiction to this theory was John Breeze, a fifty year old air-raid warden, who, on duty on the very first night of the war, broke into a pub on Meadowhall Road and helped himself to beer and cigarettes. When he appeared in the Police Court he said he had been alone at his post and felt frightened. The prosecutor, asking for the case to be committed to the Quarter Sessions, said that the court would be urged to impose a heavy sentence, pointing out that in France the death sentence had been introduced for such offences. Breeze must have been extremely relieved when, at the Sessions, he was bound over for twelve months, the Recorder accepting his story that he had lost his nerve.

The blackout provided excellent cover for armed robber Francis Fitzpatrick who, in November, 1939, held up a pawnbroker as he was cashing up in his shop on Penistone road. Pointing a revolver at him, Fitzpatrick snatched forty pounds in cash and disappeared into the darkness. A week later he entered a Duke Street shop and, again at gunpoint, robbed a female assistant of fourteen pounds, saying, "Hand over the paper money, sister." Fitzpatrick, a deserter from the army, was arrested in a cafe in The Wicker and sentenced to seven years penal servitude at Leeds Assizes after pleading with the judge to be given a chance and allowed to join the navy.

Another blackout raid, in March, 1941, produced a haul of fur coats worth £2,960. Using a master key, thieves entered the shop of John Atkinson Ltd. in High Street and removed the furs to a waiting van. None of the property was ever recovered but one man was later arrested. Edgar Wattam, a Londoner, and, like many charged with serious crime during the war, an army deserter, was alleged in court to have told police that he would rather serve in Dartmoor than in His Majesty's Forces. Mr. Justice Croom-Johnson commented, "Perhaps I can oblige him" – and gave Wattam, aged thirty-two, seven years.

Rumours that a man dressed in female clothing was molesting women in the Wicker-Pye Bank district led to a police statement in December, 1939 that, although four women had been attacked in the previous month, the public should not be alarmed. There had, said Supt. Woodward of Central Division, been fewer attacks on women during the blackout than in normal times. Shortly afterwards, a thirty year old railway porter was given four months hard labour after being caught in the act of assaulting a nurse in Corporation Street.

Another negative product of the darkened streets concerned vandalism on telephone boxes. The Telephone Manager, speaking in November, 1944, said that cases of theft and damage in public telephone boxes had increased considerably since the beginning of the war. In that year alone, he said, there had been one hundred and fifty cases, and the damage, much of which was wanton, was not confined to any particular district of the city.

The air raids which had been anticipated in Sheffield since the declaration of war in September 1939 did not materialize until December of the following year. When they came they wreaked a trail of death and destruction all over the city. But, while the emergency services began the task of clearing up the damage, less public-spirited individuals set out to prey upon the dead, the bereaved and the homeless by looting their property. Not only shops and commercial premises were targets for the looters – so too were the many houses, which had been evacuated by occupiers unable to remove the belongings. One victim, whose home had been bombed, described in a letter to the *Telegraph and Independent* how looters had removed everything which was usable from the ruins, including all the slates from outbuildings. "It certainly does seem a terrible thing," he wrote, "that persons who have lost almost everything in this manner should be stripped of even the last bits by these scroungers."

Between December 13th, 1940 and February 25th, 1941 there were 341 reported cases of looting in Sheffield and for weeks after the blitz the police worked special duties, keeping vulnerable property under observation. In spite of severe penalties which could be imposed for looting under the Defence Regulations – including the death penalty and penal servitude for life – a significant number of people seemed to find the temptation of unguarded property too strong to resist.

At Leeds Assizes in March, 1940 seventeen people were charged with the most serious offences of looting, and on the first day alone six men were imprisoned for a total of thirty-six years by Mr. Justice Oliver. Sentencing Frederick Fountain to ten years, the judge said: "In every case you have preyed on the shattered houses of the poor. You gave up a job of seven to nine pounds a week because the looting paid you better." Fountain, together with two teenagers, one a thirteen year old juvenile, had stolen clothing, household effects, cutlery, toys and carpets from houses damaged by bombs. At one house, where a woman was trapped alive for two days under wreckage, he had stolen property while the rescuers were at work. When arrested he had tried to put all the blame on the thirteen year old boy.

A Sheffield soldier who had systematically broken into temporarily vacated houses in the city was given seven years, while two sappers with the Royal Engineers Bomb Disposal Squad each received five years. They had taken food, cigars and jewellery from bombed shops which they were in the process of demolishing. The entire demolition force had earlier been paraded and warned of the stiff penalties for looting. Speaking of "the enormous extent of looting in Sheffield after the air raids," Mr. Justice Oliver said the offence was made worse by the fact that the defendants were soldiers.

"Atrocious and abominable" was the way the judge described the case of William Hague, a thirty-one year old coal bagger who stole clothes and £4/10/0d in cash from the homes of people killed during an air raid. Said to be a persistent thief who was fond of drink, he was imprisoned for five years.

On the second day of the Assizes the judge issued a warning to would-be looters. Commenting on the wholesale scale of some of the cases he had heard, of men who had given up well paid jobs of national importance to take up looting – predominately the homes of poor people – he said: "There are apparently still people who do not appreciate the seriousness of looting. The law puts these looters in the same category as murderers. The day may well be approaching when a case may arise in which they will be treated as such." Earlier he had sent several Sheffield youths to Borstal for three years and had sentenced two brothers, described by Det. Sgt. Boyden of Sheffield C.I.D. as "idle, dirty liars with no sense of honesty" to five and four years imprisonment.

Out of 371 cases of looting reported, 144 were detected, the less serious being dealt with at the Quarter Sessions and Juvenile Court. It seems, however, that not all cases of looting were reported, for police recovered many articles for which owners could not be traced.

Besides looters, other criminals were quick to capitalize on the aftermath of the Blitz. In April, 1941 it was reported that men with criminal records were seizing on the need for fire-watchers in Sheffield as a means to commit further crimes. A circular issued by the Chamber of Commerce stated: "The freedom with which watchers are permitted to patrol buildings provides crooks with first class opportunities for theft." It was recommended that applicants' credentials be thoroughly checked.

A more sophisticated ploy brought the name of Sam Garvin, former leader of the Park Brigade, into the news in 1941. Garvin and three other men appeared in the Police Court after organising a fund, disguised as a raffle, in aid of a survivor of the air raid which destroyed Marples Hotel in

Fitzalan Square. Four thousand tickets for the 'Fund of Buller Morton' had been printed and over half had been sold in public houses. Walter 'Buller' Morton was one of the defendants and he told the magistrates he had been in the Marples when it was hit and suffered leg and shoulder wounds. The prosecutor told the court: "This kind of thing closely approximates to what the Americans call a racket." But the luck which had carried Garvin to five acquittals, including one of murder, during the gang days did not desert him now. He and his three co-accused, all of whom were believed to have profited considerably from the 'fund', were each fined thirty shillings.

A matter of prime concern to the Government throughout the war was the maintenance of public morale, and anyone thought to be undermining this was hastily prosecuted. Substantial fines or prison sentences were imposed in numerous local cases where people refused to work and criticism of the Government or the armed forces proved just as costly as it had in the First World War.

A Co-op cafe manager who remarked to his cook that the navy treated people like dogs found himself in court in 1942. Charged with 'making statements likely to cause alarm and despondency', he was also alleged to have said to three servicemen in his cafe, on the morning after the Sheffield Blitz, "I told you so. This is nothing to what you will get. Next time he will use gas." Claiming to have been quoted out of context and to be totally behind the war effort, he was fined twenty pounds.

Oswald Skidmore, a forty-eight year old electrical engineer, was given three months hard labour for causing great annoyance in his place of employment by giving a Nazi salute on his arrival each morning, and goose-stepping up and down the workshop. He had declared that one German was worth five Englishmen, that Russia and Germany were better countries than Britain, and that one thing this country needed was a revolution. Skidmore, who had earlier been deported from Australia after serving seven years for attempted murder and supplying cocaine, was not a member of any political party. He had one son who was a prisoner of war and another serving in the army.

Summing up, in 1940, in the trial of four Sheffield men accused of stealing medical cards, Mr. Justice Cassels told the jury: "We are not engaged in a political trial." This did not deter one of the men, Frederick Jackson, from giving a ten minute speech, which climaxed with the cry, "Long live the Fourth International!" Jackson had engineered a scheme in which an orderly at a Medical Board office in Sheffield stole medical cards and official stationery. The cards were sent to the headquarters of the Fourth International, a left wing organisation, whose members, by forging false medical details, could use them to evade military service. Jackson, who lodged in Filey Street, told the court that the social and economic system was out of date and war was inevitable. He said he considered any act which strengthened the working class and the Fourth International was justified, although he did not expect sympathy from a capitalist court.

The orderly who stole the cards was Arthur Carford, of Portobello Road, Sheffield. He had come to the notice of New Scotland Yard as early as 1922, when he was suspected of passing arms to Sinn Fein. Considered by the police to be a dangerous revolutionary, Carford had been expelled from the Communist Party for disruptive activities and terrorism in connection with the unemployed.

Jackson and Carford were found guilty of conspiracy to defeat the purposes of the National Services (Armed Forces) Act. Sentencing Jackson to two years imprisonment the judge said that with the country at war it was difficult to see how his actions could have assisted the working classes. Carford, said by his counsel to have 'gone straight' for some years – he had become an air raid warden in 1937 – was sentenced to eighteen months.

By 1941, when rationing and shortages began to grip, an alternative economy was already thriving in many parts of the country. In Sheffield, as in other large cities, profiteering, pilfering and black market offences came to light in increasing numbers as legitimate supplies failed to satisfy public demand.

Numerous local shopkeepers were fined for selling food at excessive prices, although the average fine of about eight pounds did little to deter. This sentencing policy seems to have been common throughout the country, for in June, 1941 there was a protest in Parliament that those engaged in profiteering on food and dealing in black market goods were being allowed to get away with it virtually unscathed.

Pilfering from employers was widespread, with provision merchants particularly vulnerable. In November, 1942 fifteen Sheffield people were charged with illegally dealing in rationed food, stolen from Joseph Walker & Sons of North Church Street. A warehouseman was imprisoned for six months for stealing ninety pounds worth of butter, lard, salmon and bacon. Twelve employees of the firm were fined for obtaining controlled goods, although they had paid for all that they had received.

Hoarding food in suspicious circumstances brought six months sentences for three local men in 1942. Police found a large quantity of foodstuffs – 158 pounds of sugar, seventy-seven tins of tomatoes and ninety-one tins of milk – when they visited a stable on Rutland Street. The stable was alleged to be a clearing house for stolen food, which was driven in and out on carts topped up by rubbish. One of the accused claimed he had been collecting the food for needy people.

In another case of 'acquiring more food than his household needed for a four week period', an Abbeydale Road garage proprietor was fined twenty pounds. A search of his home by police revealed 113 pounds of onions, a milk churn half-full of fish oil and 205 tins or bottles of other rationed foodstuffs. A pub landlord, convicted of selling sugar and tea, did not escape so lightly. He was imprisoned for twelve months and fined £250.

Selling stockings and underwear resulted in six months imprisonment for an Indian, Mohamed Sharif, of Carver Street, and at the same hearing nineteen women were each fined five pounds for buying the goods. Another man was imprisoned after 216 baby sets and thirty-one raincoats were found in his loft, and fines totalling £510 were imposed on a Manchester woman for supplying dresses without coupons. She had called on large houses in the Fulwood and Ranmoor areas, offering good quality garments for sale. At one house she sold five dresses for eighty-four pounds. The purchasers in these transactions appear not to have been prosecuted.

Refusal to explain where he had obtained £200 worth of cutlery, found in his garage, led to a hundred pound fine on a Fulwood man in early 1944. Six months later he was fined £500 for a similar offence, admitting on this occasion that it was "black market stuff." In the same year a different type of racket was smashed when Sheffield police, acting in collaboration with Scotland Yard's Flying Squad, arrested three men who had sold twelve hundred dolls from rented premises in Cambridge Arcade, Moorhead. The dolls, worth only 2/6d each, had been sold for a pound and one of the men told police they had come to Sheffield after hearing that the city was paved with gold and war workers, earning high wages, would "pay through the nose" to buy toys for their children.

One of the more enterprising local efforts to capitalise on war shortages came to grief when Alexander John Rutter was imprisoned for three years in 1942. Described by the judge as a "dangerous rogue and a menace to honest business people", Rutter bought 150,000 scrap razor blades from a city manufacturer on the understanding that they were useless for shaving. He paid ten pounds for the load, rented premises and employed staff to pack the blades in specially printed wrappers, marked 'Sheffield Made Safety Razor Blades'.

The thriving black market in razor blades caused particular concern to the Price Control Committee. A spokesman told the *Sheffield Telegraph* in 1943: "The racket in the sale of razor blades must, and will, be stamped out." It was an optimistic threat which had not a hope of being carried out.

Of all the black market and profiteering offences, those involving food and clothing coupons seem to have attracted the least consistency with regard to the sentences imposed. A grocer, prosecuted for attempting to illegally obtain food coupons, was fined £160. A man whose house, in Myrtle Road, was found to contain 11,000 coupons was fined nine pounds. Accepting illicit coupons cost an Attercliffe draper forty-five pounds, while sixty-three women who had bought goods with the coupons were each fined a pound. The stiffest sentence of all concerned a fifty year old blind man, who appeared at the Quarter Sessions in 1943 accused of selling his personal allocation of clothing coupons. He told the court he had believed he was entitled to sell his own property. He was imprisoned for a month while the woman who bought the coupons off him was fined five pounds.

As the war progressed, so too did the black market. Despite warnings to the public and appeals to their sense of morality – like that of the Price Control Committee spokesman who stated: "Any person buying in the black market is playing the enemy's game for him" – many people were quite happy to pay high prices for low quality goods, especially consumer goods. In early 1942 the Chairman of the Price Control Committee reported: "Black markets in cosmetics and silk stockings are difficult to suppress because women are so anxious to get the articles that they will pay any price asked for, without complaining." He cited a case where a cheap brand of rouge, worth threepence, was misrepresented as a good brand, complete with label, and sold at 1/10d. The main difficulty, he said, was that so few complaints were made.

However, profiteering and black market activities in Sheffield were less professionally organised than in other large Northern cities. In Manchester in 1942 a large scale racket involving 97,000 forged coupons resulted in the prosecution of twenty-two people, and in the following year seven men and three women were given prison sentences for black market dealings to the value of £42,000. In Leeds the thriving black market in cloth and other goods was highly organised and based on ready cash, without the complication of coupons. Liverpool, as a seaport through which goods were constantly on the move, presented many opportunities for theft and, as in Leeds, the black market was reputedly run by an established gang of villains. By comparison with these cities, black market activity in Sheffield was small-time, so much so that in January, 1945 Supt. Allen of the city police could tell the *Telegraph*: "There are no large black market gangs working in Sheffield."

The most serious local crime of the war years, in terms of the value of property reported stolen, was not directly related to the war situation. At lunchtime on February 10th, 1943 two men, posing as workmen, gained entry to the home of Mr. Mark Green, in Collegiate Crescent. Once inside they bound and gagged two maids, broke open a safe, and stole jewellery worth £3,500, plus £10,500 in cash. A month later Henry Aarons, an army deserter from London, appeared in Sheffield Police Court and was identified by one of the maids. The defence challenged the existence of cash in the safe, but Mr. Green maintained that the amount he had reported stolen was correct and that he had won it gambling. If the judge or jury had any doubts about this claim they were not made public, but Aarons was found not guilty of robbery with violence and was given eighteen months for 'larceny to the value of more than five pounds'. The following year a Leicester man was charged with involvement in the raid, but was discharged after one of the maids could not identify him.

The last months of the war saw the biggest murder hunt in the city for years. On January 13th, 1945, Eleanor Hammerton, aged seventy-nine, was found battered to death in her small drapery shop on Ecclesall Road. A spinster, she lived alone and had no close friends or relatives. A jemmy was found in the shop, which had been ransacked.

On March 28th, after ten weeks of intense police investigation, a man arrested for a warehouse burglary surprised officers by making a full confession to the murder. Ernest Bramham, thirty-three, a known criminal who had served one period of penal servitude for unlawful wounding, said that he had gone into the old lady's shop and asked to buy a shirt. As she reached for one he had hit her with his jemmy. He took 15/- from a drawer and, having misplaced the jemmy, hit her again with a poker. He stole £4/10/0d from the back room then left the shop, went for a drink, and spent the afternoon at Hyde Park dog track. At his trial the following month Bramham was convicted of murder and sentenced to death. Two days before he was due to hang he was certified insane and ordered to Broadmoor. He was later released and returned to Sheffield.

Throughout the war years there were frequent forecasts that, once peace was restored, a great increase in crime would sweep throughout Britain. In 1943 the Lord Mayor of Sheffield, Councillor H. E. Bridgewater, made one such forecast, while stating his concern at the steady increase in local juvenile crime since the war had begun.

The greater proportion of those who appeared before the city Juvenile Court were placed on probation, although the birch was quite frequently imposed in the early years. In 1941 a thirteen year old boy who had obtained 11/6d from a man by claiming he could get him cigarettes was ordered to receive six strokes. By the end of the war the mood of magistrates seems to have mellowed: six boys charged in May, 1945 with breaking into a barracks and stealing 1,200 rounds of ammunition, only 200 of which were recovered, were each fined a pound. The chairman, Mr. B. Pye-Smith, said: "The citizens of Sheffield ought to know there are a thousand rounds of ammunition being handed round among schoolchildren in the city. It is a miracle no one has been killed or injured."

The gloomy forecasts of what lay ahead were proved to have some accuracy. When the publication of Chief Constables' Reports resumed in 1945 the number of indictable crimes in Sheffield had increased by twenty-eight per cent over the 1940 figures, while the value of property stolen in the city had risen from £17,098 to £50,673 – a rise of 196 per cent. Commenting on the increase, Mr. G. S. Lowe, who had succeeded Major James as Chief Constable in 1941, blamed the abnormal social conditions which had prevailed during the war, and particularly during 1946. He said: "The difficulties of re-habilitation in civil life for ex members of His Majesty's Forces, the general slackening of moral standards which history proves to be the inevitable sequel to every great war, the persistent shortage of goods and the vulnerability of so many temporary and damaged buildings are naturally reflected in the crime statistics . . . . Having regard to the difficulties of the times, the shortage of police officers, black market activities etc, the figures might have been far worse."

Two year later, in 1948, reporting a decrease in the number of crimes committed, Mr. Lowe told the Watch Committee: "While Sheffield, in common with other large cities, has more crime than we like to see, I am glad to say that there has been no sensational crime wave so far as this city is concerned and I deplore the tendency of some people to exaggerate the situation." The worst effects of the war had passed. The crisis was over.

POST-WAR CRIME: Enter the Professionals

Although the crime epidemic which had been prophesied did not fully materialize in the immediate post-war years, the late 1940s and early '50s saw an increase in planned, professional crime in the city. In a lorry hijack in 1947 two-and-a-quarter million cigarettes – worth £8,000 – were stolen by a Leeds gang, aided by two local men. Nine members of the gang were later given sentences of up to seven years. An outbreak of post office breaking in the winter of 1952-3, in which safes were blown with explosives, came to an end with the arrest of a Sheffield man in early 1953. He had a large number of National Insurance stamps in his possession and was found to have blown safes in many different parts of the country,

A series of house breakings and burglaries in late 1953 and early '54 caused suspicion to fall upon William Hart, a man who had only recently been released from a ten year sentence. Hart was a methodical burglar who lived with a woman in Leeds and pretended that he worked night shifts in Sheffield. He travelled over in the early evening and usually went to the cinema, staying until the last performance and then walking to the scene of his intended operations. After breaking into several houses each night he returned to the city centre, cleaned himself up in a public toilet, breakfasted at a cafe, and returned to Leeds by bus. Police investigations led to Hart's description being circulated to attendants at city cinemas and public conveniences and he was soon arrested after being recognised at 5.30 a.m. one morning in Fitzalan Square toilets. At the April Quarter Sessions he admitted many offences in Sheffield, the West Riding and Lancashire, and was sentenced to seven years preventive detention.

An attempt to defraud Vernons Pools brought five years imprisonment for Lucien De Pontino, a motor mechanic of Polish origin, in 1954. De Pontino visited Sheffield Midland Station and picked up a pools mailbag. He removed an envelope and took the mailbag to Liverpool, where he inserted a winning forecast after the football results were announced. He then placed the coupon and envelope back in the mailbag, which he re-sealed and left on the station platform to be collected and delivered to Vernons. For some time pools companies had been suspicious of coupons bearing De Pontino's address in Wayland Road, Sharrow, and, following investigations, he was charged with attempting to obtain £60,357 by forgery. De Pontino, who, like many fraudsters claimed a colourful background, told Sheffield police he had been in a German concentration camp and a Russian prison camp, from where he had escaped to work, first as a British spy in Hungary, and later as a cinema attendant in Yugoslavia. He had become a naturalised British subject in 1949 and arrived in Sheffield in 1953, having assumed another name.

Increased thefts of metal led to the formation of a special squad of detectives in 1952. In the first four months of the squad's existence fifty-five people were arrested and police attention became focussed on the business premises of a registered scrap dealer who was engaged in receiving stolen metal. At his trial in July, 1952 the metal squad's conduct was severely criticized by Mr. G. D. Roberts Q.C., defending. He claimed that Detective Inspector Alfred Longmore, the officer in charge of the case, had "transcended all the principles of fairness in police investigations." Mr. Justice Oliver said he did not share such views and sentenced the sixty year old dealer to four years and his two sons, aged twenty-seven and twenty-eight, to eighteen months each. Two months after the father was released from prison in 1955 he and his sons were again charged with similar offences, but were acquitted after a four day trial.

In another trial, scrap dealer Byron Heselwood was sent to prison for five years and four of his employees for lesser terms, after being convicted of a number of offences of conspiracy and receiving metal stolen from Sheffield steelworks. It was stated that on the proceeds of crime Heselwood bought land and two farms in Derbyshire, while continuing to live in a small house in Candow Street, Attercliffe. The prosecution alleged that his scrapyard was a "thieves' kitchen, an ever open door to which thieves could bring their stolen property." Thirteen policemen received commendations for their work in the investigation.

Violence in the course of burglary brought a five year sentence for Charles Rhodes Currie, aged fifty-eight, who was told by Mr. Justice Hallett in 1947: "Far too many householders, caretakers and watchmen are being assaulted." Currie, who had a record going back almost forty years, is interesting, not because of this offence – he had assaulted two men who disturbed him breaking into a factory – but more through the part he played in a murder investigation twenty years earlier.

In September, 1927, P.C. George Gutteridge, an Essex policeman, was shot four times in the head while on duty. Two of the bullets had been fired through his eyes – it was thought that his killer believed the superstition that the eyes of a dying man photograph the last thing he sees. A large scale hunt for the killer or killers was undertaken, but police had no clues as to identity until, by a curious twist of fate, Charles Currie, living at the time in Douglas Terrace, Sheffield, was apprehended for a motoring offence committed weeks earlier in the city. Panicking, and anxious not to be implicated in a murder charge, Currie asked to speak to Percy Sillitoe, then Chief Constable, and told him that the killers of P.C. Gutteridge were two men named Frederick Kennedy and William Browne. After the murder they had driven to Sheffield and asked Currie, with whom they were familiar, to look after the revolver with which they had shot the policeman. Currie had wisely refused.

Kennedy and Browne were soon arrested, tried and hanged, while Currie received a £2,000 reward from the *News of the World*. Criminal history has preserved the names of Kennedy and Browne as brutal murderers, while Currie, the man responsible for their capture, achieved fleeting celebrity status and was soon forgotten. In the newspaper report of his case in 1947 the Gutteridge murder was not even mentioned.

On July 8th, 1959, the residents and passers-by in a Sheffield back street witnessed at firsthand crime London-style. At 10.15 on that Friday morning an Austin car travelled along Woodburn Road, Attercliffe. On hire to Williams Deacons Bank and driven by ex-speedway rider Albert Harvey, the car carried two bank employees and over £51,000 in cash.

The Woodburn Road bank car robbery. From: The Star, July 8th, 1959.

Suddenly, a light grey Jaguar overtook the bank car, forcing it to a halt on the nearside kerb. Six men leapt from the Jaguar, smashed the Austin's windows, and snatched £49,500 in banknotes from the boot. Leaving behind £1,900 in coin, they jumped into a Morris van which had driven up, and departed. The Jaguar, stolen a month earlier in London, was abandoned, as was the van which was found close to the scene of the robbery. The money was never seen again.

On November 19th, 1959, at Sheffield Assizes, three London men – Ronald Strongman, Patrick Moore and James William Jennings – pleaded not guilty to taking part in the robbery. The police were led to Jennings, a street trader, after a witness noted the number of the van used in the raid, and it was found to have been hired in London. The keys to the stolen

Jaguar were also found in Jennings' home. He admitted hiring the van, which he said he had delivered to some other men, who wanted it to transport television sets. He told police: "I could cry. I've been run in for this for eighty pounds and the others are sharing fifty grand. You know who they are. Don't ask me anything more. I've been chivved once. I don't want my throat cut."

Strongman, a thirty-nine year old general dealer and father of five children, was identified by one of the bank employees. He denied ever having been to Sheffield, claiming he had been in Brighton, where he collected his baby from hospital on the morning that the robbery took place. The hospital had initially confirmed his story, but then said that they had made a mistake and that he had been to the hospital on the following day. Moore, who described himself as a bookmakers' assistant, brought two witnesses who told the court that they had conducted betting business with him in Smithfield Market, London on the morning of July 8th. Moore was identified as having taken part in the robbery by a resident of Woodburn Road.

After a trial lasting five days, all three men were found guilty. Mr. Justice Thesinger told them: "Sentence must be apt, seeing that this capital sum, free of tax, is available for their colleagues." He added: "I must also take into account that young people may be impressed by this type of crime." Strongman, who declared to the court: "As God is my judge I was never in Sheffield", and Moore were each sentenced for fourteen years for robbery with violence. Jennings, convicted of the lesser charges of being an accessory and conspiracy, was given five years. The judge told him that it was unfortunate that he had not turned Queen's Evidence. Had he done so, the whole gang would no doubt have been convicted, for the police arrested all six men whom they believed to have been involved in the robbery, but had to release three owing to witnesses being unable to identify them.

The Woodburn Road bank car robbery took less than fifty seconds from beginning to end. For one of the convicted robbers, at least, the sudden wealth was to be of no benefit. Shortly after his arrival at Armley Prison, Ronald Strongman was found dead in his cell. He had committed suicide.

Two years after the Woodburn Road robbery, another Londoner named James Jennings received the longest prison sentence every imposed in a Sheffield court. On February 21st, 1961 James Henry Jennings was sentenced to twenty-two years for his part in a series of burglaries and armed robberies at houses in the Sheffield and West Riding areas. His partner – the pair were nicknamed the 'Robin Hood Bandits' on account of the type of hats they wore when raiding – was Eric Mangle, a Sheffield man, who received nineteen years.

Jennings was already on the run after escaping from custody in Bedford, where he had been arrested for an £8,000 post office robbery, when he met up with Mangle, whose criminal abilities were well known to local police. In a six month period they stole cash and property to the value of £27,500. In one raid on a city home a woman was robbed at the point of a shotgun of ivory carvings worth nearly £5,000, and in another, jewellery valued at over £4,000 was stolen from the home of a magistrate.

On Christmas Eve, 1960 the 'Robin Hood Bandits' went to a house in Cavendish Road, Nether Edge, the home of a sixty year old potato merchant and his wife. Despite both robbers being armed, the householder, Mr. Stanley Taylor, and a guest, Mr. Peter Lawton, tackled them, whereupon Mangle shot Mr. Lawton in the thigh and Jennings assaulted Mr. Taylor with the barrel of his gun. The pair then departed in a hurry, leaving behind their distinctive headgear.

Jennings and Mangle, both aged twenty-four, were arrested in their beds in a Redcar flat on New Years Day, 1961. In the flat was a sawn-off shotgun, a loaded pistol, an automatic Colt and a revolver. They had been traced after Sheffield police circulated the registration number of a car they had hired from a city firm. Brought to Sheffield in chains, they were still chained when they appeared before the magistrates and were committed to the Assizes.

Eric Mangle's nineteen year sentence was reduced to twelve years on appeal. In September, 1964, while working in the laundry at Dartmoor Prison, he escaped, along with three other convicts, by overpowering a guard and going over the prison wall. On the run for eight weeks, he was given a consecutive six month sentence when recaptured. He was eventually released in 1970 after serving nine-and-a-half years.

Between the end of the war in 1945 and the abolition of the death penalty in 1965 there were thirty-four murders in Sheffield. In several instances more than one victim was killed by the same person and a substantial majority of victims were killed by either a parent, spouse or cohabitee. While some of those indicted for murder were found guilty of the lesser charge of manslaughter, in every murder case investigated by Sheffield police during this period the perpetrator was detected.

Unusual circumstances surrounded the killing of Edith Simmonite, aged twenty-seven, found dead in a derelict outbuilding in Bridge Street on March 8th, 1947. A known prostitute, she had been strangled with a scarf. For weeks the police investigated without success, until William Smedley, a resident of the West Bar Hostel, telephoned the C.I.D., saying he would tell them the identity of the murderer for ten pounds. When questioned he claimed that the person was an Irishman, living in Rhyl. He was given three pounds, told he could have the remainder when the killer was found, and was driven to North Wales, where he said he had arranged to meet the man. On the journey Smedley confessed that he had strangled Edith Simmonite.

At his trial at Leeds Assizes in July, 1947, Smedley, a thirty-eight year old colliery worker, pleaded not guilty to murder. He admitted strangling Simmonite, with whom he had associated for some months, saying that he lost control after she told him that she had venereal disease. However, his defence collapsed when the court learned that Smedley had visited a clinic in November, 1946 and had named Simmonite as the person from whom he had contracted the disease. Found guilty and sentenced to death, he collapsed in the dock when the black cap was placed on the judge's head.

William Smedley was hanged at Armley Prison, Leeds, on August 14th, 1947. There were no sightseers outside the prison and the execution merited only brief mention in the Sheffield newspapers. His was the last death sentence carried out in a case from Sheffield.

Melanie Birch was another Sheffield prostitute who was strangled to death, in High Hazels Park, Darnall in 1954. Born in Russia and a former nurse in the Russian Army, she had arrived in Sheffield in 1920 after forming a relationship with a Sergeant Birch of the York & Lancs. Regiment, in her homeland, shortly after the First World War. He later died and 'Russian Edna', as she was widely known in city public houses, resorted to prostitution. Only hours before she died, at the age of fifty-two, she had called at the Court House and paid a five pound fine imposed a week earlier for soliciting.

A twenty-four year old lorry driver of Hall Road, Handsworth was arrested the day after 'Russian Edna's' body was found. He admitted meeting her in the Sportmans Inn, Cambridge Street and taking a taxi to High Hazels Park, where he gave her a pound. He claimed that she had demanded another pound, threatening to scream if he did not pay, and he had put his hand over her mouth to stop her. He said that he thought she was sulking when she made "queer sounds".

Mr. Justice Donovan, summing up at Leeds Assizes, suggested to the jury that the defendant knew what he had done. He said: "This was not an act of love-making on that night. It was an act of lust from beginning to end. He was there to get his money's worth." After considering their verdict for one and a quarter hours the jury found the man not guilty of murder, but guilty of manslaughter. Rather surprisingly, in view of his earlier comments, the judge sentenced him to only twelve months imprisonment.

For centuries murder cases from Sheffield, along with other serious charges, were heard at the Assize Courts of York, and later Leeds. The opening of Sheffield Assizes on June 23rd, 1955 was greeted with great enthusiasm in the city, a crowd of between three and four thousand people gathering in Castle Street to greet the Lord Chief Justice, Lord Goddard, when he arrived to perform the opening ceremony. The first murder case to be heard in the city concerned a local woman who was found unfit to

Castle Street on June 23rd, 1955. The opening of Sheffield Assizes.
Photo: Sheffield Newspapers Ltd.

plead to the murder of her seven year old daughter. She was ordered to be detained during Her Majesty's Pleasure.

Up until 1957 anyone convicted of murder faced a mandatory death sentence, which could be respited to life imprisonment only by the intervention of the Home Secretary. This occurred in a number of instances, notably in 1953 when a married couple were both convicted of the murder of their newborn baby, and in another case two years later, where an unmarried mother had gassed her thirteen month old daughter.

On March 21st, 1957 the Homicide Bill, restricting application of the death penalty to just six types of murder, received the Royal Assent. The death penalty was retained only in cases of a convicted (but reprieved) murderer committing another murder on a different occasion, and for the following classes of capital murder: killing in the course of theft; killing while resisting or avoiding arrest; killing of prison officers or people assisting them; killing of police officers and people assisting them; murder by shooting or causing explosions. Life imprisonment was prescribed for all non-capital murders.

At the time of the Royal Assent being received, six people were under sentence of death in the country. Two of the six were from Sheffield: Henry Barker, aged fifty-nine, who had killed his seventy year old sister with a hammer at their home in Wallace Road, and Mahsen Abdul Gawit, an Arab labourer convicted after stabbing a Pakistani to death during an argument at a house in Dundas Road, Tinsley. For Barker and Gawit the Bill proved extremely fortuitous – both were due to be executed the following week, but were reprieved.

Although William Smedley was the last Sheffield man to be hanged, in 1947, there were several later death sentences passed at Sheffield Assizes, and carried out at Leeds, in respect of murders committed outside the city. The last such case from the city courts was that of Bernard Hugh Walden, hanged for the shooting of two students at Rotherham Technical College, where he was a lecturer.

Walden, aged thirty-three, had become friendly with twenty-one year old Joyce Moran, but when he proposed marriage she rejected him. On April 7th, 1959, after taking an evening lecture, he shot her and her boyfriend, Neil Saxton, with a 9mm Luger and promptly went on the run. He visited various parts of the country, buying a shotgun on his travels. He had the shotgun by his side when arrested in Reading, after being spotted sleeping on a park bench by a police constable. Walden pleaded diminished responsibility but was convicted of capital murder and hanged at Leeds on August 14th, 1959.

The murder of three men in the East House pub, Spital Hill, might never have happened had it not been for the religious beliefs of the killer, Mohammed Ismail. Ismail, a thirty-two year old Somalian who had lived in Sheffield for the previous six years, became depressed and wished to end his life. His religion forbade this, on pain of eternal damnation, and, so he later claimed, voices in his head told him to go out on a bloody rampage and force someone to kill him, so that he could die without being damned.

At 10.45 p.m. on New Year's Day, 1960, as a group of seven young men sat in the East House's crowded bar, drinking and singing to the piano, Ismail took out a loaded Smith & Wesson pistol and fired five shots at them. Twenty-one year old steelworker Mick McFarlane died instantly, shot through the chest; his friends Tom Owen and Fred Morris died soon afterwards. Mick McFarlane's brother, Don, was shot in the head; he spent three months unconscious and three years in hospital and was left severely disabled.

After shooting the men Ismail left the bar and went to the pub's outside toilet, where the police arrested him minutes later. At Sheffield Assizes on February 25th, 1960 the jury took only fifteen minutes to find Ismail unfit to plead, after being told by the Medical Officer of Leeds Prison, where he had been held on remand, that there was unmistakeable evidence that he was insane. Ismail sat impassively in the dock, his wrists manacled. He

East House pub, Spital Hill. Scene of the shootings of January 1st, 1960.
Photo: Andrew C. Smith.

was said to believe that evil voices spoke to him out of the electricity system and, while in Leeds, he had smashed lightbulbs in order to stop the voices reaching him. Mr. Justice Edmund Davies ordered him to be kept in strict custody for the duration of Her Majesty's Pleasure.

In January, 1984 a feature article by Ian Macgill in *The Star* revealed that in April, 1962, only twenty-two months after being sentenced, Mohammed Ismail was released from Broadmoor Hospital and deported to Somalia. The survivors of the shooting were reported to be stunned by this news, none more so than Don McFarlane, who, because he had sustained his injuries prior to the introduction of the Criminal Injuries Compensation Board, received no compensation whatsoever. The day after this article appeared, a former acquaintance of Ismail's who had known him in Somalia and in Sheffield, informed *The Star* that Ismail was shot and killed in his homeland in the late 1960s, after murdering several villagers. If this account was true his perverse death wish had at last come to fruition.

In 1961 there were four murders in Sheffield. All four victims were women, three of them killed by men with whom they had formed relationships, and in each of these three cases the killer was quickly arrested. The fourth murder, that of a seventy year old spinster, caused the biggest manhunt in Sheffield since the war.

The Miss Music murder. The body of 70 year old spinster, Ethel Jones, is removed from her home in Ellesmere Road, December 22nd, 1961.
Photo: Sheffield Newspapers Ltd.

Ethel Jones, a former nun and music teacher, lived alone in Ellesmere Road, Pitsmoor. Rumoured to be wealthy, and to keep large amounts of money at home, she was found strangled there on December 22nd, 1961. Continuous enquiries, involving 250 police officers working eighteen hours a day, led to 5,600 houses being visited and over 32,000 people interviewed before the 'Miss Music' murder, as it became known, was solved.

Detectives even prayed together for help in catching the killer. In a unique scene a hundred officers took part in a service conducted at the murder headquarters, All Saints Church, and Detective Chief Superintendent George Carnill, the man leading the hunt, read out from the Bible. A week later, electrician's mate, Brian Phillips, of Lyons Road, was arrested.

Phillips, twenty years old and recently married – his wife was expecting their first child – told the police: "I didn't mean to kill her. Will my wife get to know?" He had no previous convictions and had gone to the home of Miss Jones, whom he knew, supposedly to obtain the house number for his aunt, who wished to send the old lady a Christmas card. He told police he was drunk and she became alarmed, whereupon he grabbed her by the throat and banged her head on the floor. He then ransacked the house and stole £4/3/0d.

Had Phillips been found guilty of capital murder – killing in the furtherance of theft – he would have been sentenced to hang. However, the jury at Leeds Assizes found him guilty only of the non-capital crime and he was sentenced to life imprisonment. In Miss Jones' will, published shortly afterwards, she left her estate of £2,500 to charity.

THE RHINO WHIP AFFAIR

For most of the immediate post-war period Sheffield City Police force operated under strength. Whereas in the 1930s there had been dozens of applications for every vacancy, the post-war employment situation, and poor police pay by comparison with many jobs, caused acute recruitment problems. In 1961 the force was 112 under its establishment strength of 815 officers.

Despite this shortfall, the statistics for indictable crime committed in the city remained reasonably steady, while the detection rate between 1946 and 1963 never fell below 49 per cent, and in 1955 reached 65.83 per cent[1].

It was a drop in the detection rate in the early months of 1963 which led to the formation on March 9th of a Crime Squad, comprising seven detectives under the overall control of the head of Sheffield C.I.D., Detective Chief Superintendent George Carnill. The squad was relieved of duties concerning day-to-day crime in order to concentrate on serious offences, mainly break-ins.

In the first few days the Crime Squad achieved little in the way of immediate results and on March 14th all members attended a meeting where the necessity for long hours and devotion to the task were stressed. It is worth noting that the previous year's detection rate was 62.07 per cent, a figure eighteen per cent above the national average.

Following the meeting the Squad received information which led them to the White Horse public house in Malinda Street. There they arrested two brothers and a third man, all known criminals, and took them back to C.I.D. headquarters in Water Lane. What happened next caused the greatest furore in the history of Sheffield police, a scandal which received extensive national attention and took years for the city force to live down.

In the Conference Room at Water Lane the three arrested men were brutally and systematically assaulted by two detective constables, with an old-fashioned police truncheon and an instrument which was well known in the lower ranks of the C.I.D. as a 'rhino tail'. One of the two detectives had acquired this from among a collection of confiscated offensive weapons. He later admitted carrying it on bank escort duties and "in case of conflicts between coloured informants." The 'rhino tail' was about eight inches long, made of a gut-like material, with a plaited loop at one end.

The object of the beatings was to elicit confessions to alleged break-ins at Crookes Valley Park Cafe and the Forum Cinema. One of the arrested brothers was assaulted three times by one detective with the truncheon, once by the other with the 'rhino tail', and once by both together. He claimed to have been struck sixty or seventy blows and, like his brother and the third prisoner, received injuries comprising pronounced weals and

---

[1] In one case heard before the city magistrates in 1955, six people charged with simple larceny and receiving admitted 601 offences. This accounts for 12.62 per cent of the annual figure of 65.83 per cent.

bruises over his shoulders and buttocks. Between the assaults, numbering ten in all on the three men, one of the detectives removed his jacket and shirt. Earlier he had shown a picture of Percy Sillitoe to one of the prisoners, saying: "He cleaned Sheffield up as we're going to clean Sheffield up and we've got authority to do it." While the assaults were being committed three other members of the Crime Squad watched, including an inspector who was later alleged to have laughed as the truncheon and 'rhino tail' were used. He told the subsequent Inquiry: "You can't have kid gloves on when detecting crime."

The two brothers were charged with the offences for which they had been questioned, and appeared in court the following morning, March 15th. One of them stripped to the waist, showing his injuries to the magistrates, naming as responsible the two detectives and the inspector. Both brothers were remanded in custody, bail being opposed by the police. They were, however, granted facilities that same day for a medical examination and photographs.

After the court hearing the Chief Constable, Eric Staines, gave instructions to Chief Superintendent Carnill that full and immediate enquiries were to be made to find out exactly what had happened. A chief inspector was instructed to take statements from the Crime Squad, but, despite what was clearly a matter of urgency and concern, no statements were taken from the two detective constables for almost a week, and no other member of the Crime Squad made a statement about the incident.

The subsequent Inquiry report states that, after the assaults had occurred, "five days were spent in anxious deliberation by the Squad , concocting versions that might meet or mitigate the allegations." The main author of the concocted versions, which had the two detectives quelling a fight between the two arrested brothers and the third prisoner, whom they were supposed to have accused of 'grassing', was the detective inspector who had witnessed and, according to one of the prisoners, participated in the assaults.

On March 21st, a week after the allegations had been made in the Magistrates Court, the Crime Squad made up their pocket books. A day earlier the deputy head of the C.I.D. had made a search of the Water Lane headquarters for the truncheon and 'rhino tail'. This proved fruitless, as both had already been burned some days earlier by one of the detectives who had wielded them.

On March 27th the two detective constables were issued with summonses, alleging that on the 14th they had maliciously inflicted grievous bodily harm on the three prisoners. The case against them was brought as a private prosecution by Mr. Arthur Hewitt, the men's solicitor, as it had become clear that the Chief Constable was not willing to deal with the allegations in any way other than by internal disciplinary proceedings. When confronted with photographs of the injuries, Mr. Staines had confidently expressed the view that no officer of his force could be guilty of such conduct, and had even suggested that the injuries might be the result of flagellation between sexual perverts.

At Sheffield Magistrates Court on May 2nd, the two detective constables, aged twenty-six and thirty-one, pleaded guilty to the charges against them. The chairman of the bench, Mr. Brian C. Pye-Smith, told them that they had "grossly abused" their powers but that they would not be sent to prison in view of their excellent records. One was fined £75, the other £50, and they were ordered to share costs of £98/17/0d.

There was considerable surprise at the pleas. It later transpired that the men had been advised to plead guilty and had been led to believe by senior officers that they would not lose their jobs. However, on May 4th both men appeared before the Chief Constable and were dismissed from the force.

The *Sheffield Telegraph* had followed the assault allegations closely from their first mention in the Magistrates Court. The hearing against the two detectives attracted widespread national coverage and in the ensuing days any hopes on the part of the Chief Constable that the matter would die down were soon dispelled.

On May 8th, 'Justice', the British section of an international organisation of lawyers, headed by Lord Shawcross, a former Attorney-General, demanded an independent inquiry into the conduct and control of Sheffield Police. The demand came in a letter to Mr. Henry Brooke, the Home Secretary, and the organisation said they were disturbed that a private prosecution had to be brought by a local solicitor, instead of responsibility being taken by the local prosecuting authorities.

Similar sentiments were expressed in many quarters and a mounting campaign was fuelled on June 10th when one of the sacked detectives announced that he had written to the Home Secretary, requesting permission to appeal against his dismissal from the force, and claiming serious allegations against senior officers. He told a *Sheffield Telegraph* reporter: "I feel there has been a lot of injustice. We have been made the scapegoats." Two weeks later, when his ex-colleague, who had obtained a new job as a security officer at a city dance hall, also made an application to appeal, he said: "I feel we were sold down the river on this one. But now we are appealing it will be like a two-stage rocket to get at the truth."

Eventually, in August, the Home Secretary appointed Queen's Counsel, Mr. G. R. Swanwick and H.M. Inspector of Constabulary, Commander W. J. A. Willis to sit as a tribunal to hear the appeals of the two dismissed detective constables. The real issue, though, was the culpability of others, in particular the force's most senior officers.

The Inquiry began at Sheffield Town Hall on Monday, 9th September, 1963. Sitting in public, the tribunal heard evidence from thirty-five witnesses before the hearing was completed on its twelfth day. The evidence of the three members of the Crime Squad who had witnessed the

*Eric Staines. Chief Constable of Sheffield at the time of the Rhip Whip scandal.
Photo: Sheffield newspapers.*

assaults was marked by their adamant denials that they had seen anything untoward, in the face of what the tribunal clearly felt was overwhelming evidence to the contrary. Two of these officers, an inspector and a constable, had been allowed to resign from the force. The third, a sergeant, had been transferred from C.I.D. back to uniform after disciplinary proceedings in May. The tribunal made a number of criticisms about irregularities in the way these resignations and disciplinary proceedings had been conducted.

The report of the tribunal's findings was published in November, 1963. The two convicted detectives were found to have been justifiably dismissed from the force, although the tribunal felt that the mitigating facts had been established in essence. These were that they had been working long hours, were overtired and hungry, and were under pressure to obtain results. It was felt that the violence they used was encouraged and approved by senior officers, and that two senior officers and another detective constable were inadequately dealt with by the Chief Constable. The tribunal also felt that the two dismissed detectives aggravated their offences by putting forward a false story in the Magistrates Court, and had done this at the instigation of a senior officer.

With regard to the head of C.I.D., the tribunal reported that there was no evidence that Detective Chief Superintendent Carnill ever instigated the use of violence, but he was criticized for his failure to pursue investigations in the week after the assaults came to light. It was considered that the Chief Constable, Eric Staines, leaned far too heavily on Carnill, left too much to him and was over-influenced by him. The Chief was said to have "lived somewhat in a ivory tower, barely able to accept that the men under his command could be guilty of truly infamous conduct."

On November 6th the Watch Committee announced that the Chief Constable and Detective Chief Superintendent Carnill had been suspended. Two weeks later the retirements of Carnill and his deputy, Detective Chief Inspector Wells, were announced. George Carnill, who had been awarded the MBE in the 1963 New Years Honours List, had been in the Sheffield force since 1926 and head of C.I.D. since 1955. He had received twenty commendations and in 1958 was awarded the Queen's Police Medal, with a citation which read: "The fine example he sets is an inspiration to all those who serve under him." The irony was that Carnill had been due to retire in 1961, at the time of the 'Miss Music' murder, but had not wished to end his career with a murder unsolved. He had changed his retirement date to Spring, 1963, but the allegations against his men caused him to again postpone his departure.

The Chief Constable, Eric Staines, took over the city force in 1959 from Mr. G. E. Scott. He had progressed through the ranks, after joining the police as a constable in Leeds in 1933. A former Superintendent at the Police College, until the night of March 13th, 1963 he could have looked forward to many more years at the top. Instead, on November 20th he resigned his £4,000 a year post, his career in ruins.

Comparisons between the 'Rhino Whip Affair', as it was dubbed by the Press, and the hard-hitting methods which had smashed the Mooney and Garvin gangs in the 1920s are inevitable. There is clear evidence that the influence of Percy Sillitoe, a firm advocate of tough tactics, was still strong over three decades after he had left the city. The detective who showed the prisoners a photograph of Sillitoe on the fateful night repeated very similar sentiments to those expressed in the former Chief's autobiography, published only a few years earlier, when he gave evidence to the Inquiry. He said that, in his view, criminals were treated far too softly by the courts, that force was justified as a method of detection when normal methods failed, and that a beating was the only answer to turn a hardened criminal from a life of crime.

The Sillitoe connection was also heightened by the fact that George Carnill had served his formative years in the police force under the well-known 'gangbuster'. On November 10th the *Sunday Citizen* went so far as to state in "A report from the POLICE SCANDAL TOWN" that tough police methods in Sheffield had begun during the gang days. Harking back to happier times, when such methods were not only acceptable, but applauded, ex-Sergeant William Robinson, of 'Flying Squad' fame, was quoted as saying: "If we came out of a pub with a gang man the people used to come out of their houses and cheer us all the way to the station."

The change in attitudes between the 1920s and the 1960s was referred to by Sir Robert Mark, former Metropolitan Police Commissioner, in his autobiography, *In the Office of Constable*. He wrote that the conduct of the two detective constables and their Chief Constable was little, if at all different from the methods by which Percy Sillitoe had tamed the gangs, thus gaining the approval of Press, magistrates and public alike. Commented Sir Robert: "In 1963 he would have got the sack."

Finally, the *Sheffield Telegraph*, which had relentlessly campaigned for a full inquiry into the allegations against the police, emerged from the affair with credit. While some senior police officers had taken the view that the journalists' interest had merely been a malicious smear campaign against the police, in the end their actions were vindicated by the tribunal's report. The *Telegraph* received acclaim from all sections of the Press. There were congratulations from the national newspapers, there was praise from the International Press Institute, and the editor of the paper, Mr. D. H. Hopkinson, was named 'Journalist of the Year'. In terms of reputation it seems that the police's loss was the *Telegraph's* gain.

THE GATES OF SHEFFIELD ARE OPENED

Addressing a meeting of lawyers in Sheffield in 1968, the city Recorder, Peter Stanley Price Q.C., said: "The rates of crime in Sheffield are in the highest degree praiseworthy compared with other towns of the same size." Sheffield, he said, was the most stable and happiest city in the country.

Nevertheless, while the statistics may have been higher for Liverpool, Leeds and Manchester, there was no cause for complacency in Sheffield, where, far from going into decline, crime had more than doubled in the previous six years. Improved rail services and the city's link-up with the M1 motorway had brought new problems. In June, 1968, the *Sheffield Telegraph*, while agreeing that the city's crime rate was low in comparison to other big cities, commented: "The gates of Sheffield have been opened up, bringing an increase in certain types of crime."

One such type of crime was the illegal possession and supplying of controlled drugs. In 1966 there was a total of twenty-four convictions for drug offences in the city; in the following year, which saw the inception of a new police drug squad, there were fifty-two. The majority of prosecutions in the mid 1960s concerned amphetamines of the pep-pill variety, but by 1968 the Chief Constable, Edward Barker, was reporting: "Cannabis continues to increase in popularity and many young people in the area admit to being committed to this drug." He pointed out that a number of people had been arrested at coach and railway stations as they returned to the city, having acquired cannabis in other parts of the country.

By the early '70s the more dangerous Class A drugs (heroin, cocaine, morphine, LSD etc.) were in increasing evidence. Out of 287 drug prosecutions in 1973, twenty-one involved possession of these 'hard' drugs, compared to only three in the previous year. By 1979 possession of Class A drugs accounted for eighty-one convictions out of a total of 614 offences relating to drugs in the county.

Chemists' shops were obvious targets for the more desperate – or more criminal – 'junkie'. In June, 1974 at Sheffield Crown Court, a twenty-four year old man who was said to have "made a profession" out of breaking into chemists' shops and stealing drugs to supply to the black market, was imprisoned for five years. Caught in the act of burgling a shop in Ecclesall Road, he and an accomplice promptly swallowed handfuls of tablets. The accomplice became critically ill and spent three days in intensive care. He was later sent to prison for two years.

Another effect of improved mobility to and from Sheffield was an increase in vice. In 1965 only one prostitute was prosecuted in the city, a state of affairs which led the Chief Constable to report "In a city of nearly half a million population, it is pleasing to record that the city is relatively free from complaints of prostitution and the kindred offences associated with public decency – a remarkably good record." Five years later it was felt necessary to double the strength of the city's Vice Squad and the chairman of Sheffield and Rotherham Police Authority described the city as "fast becoming a haven for prostitutes." Seventy-five women were prosecuted for soliciting in the year, many of them from other cities, notably Nottingham and Manchester. One police raid on a house where drink was being sold illegally revealed the presence of more than a hundred people from a wide area of the country, including a number of out-of-town prostitutes.

A charge of living off immoral earnings brought a five year prison sentence in 1972 for a South American-born resident of Broomhall. Commenting on the witnesses who appeared at his four day trial, prosecuting counsel told the jury: "We have been turning over stones and watching creatures scuttle away who were unaccustomed to light."

The pornography boom of the permissive '60s brought first riches and later imprisonment for two city men who ran a flourishing business importing obscene books and magazines from Europe and the USA. Their distribution network extended from the North East to London, where they bought immunity from prosecution by bribing a corrupt officer in Scotland Yard's Obscene Publications Squad. The 'Dirty Squad', as it was known, was later to figure prominently in Old Bailey trials, where thirteen Metropolitan Police officers were imprisoned for a total of ninety-six years.

But what was possible in the capital was not so in Sheffield, and when suspicions were raised at the number of vehicles being regularly loaded and unloaded from three lock-up garages in Murray Road, Greystones, the police moved in. Two hundred thousand books and magazines, weighing six tons and with a market value estimated at £500,000, were removed from the garages in a police raid.

The two main operators were each given eighteen months imprisonment, fined £2,500 and ordered to pay £1,000 costs after pleading guilty to possessing obscene articles for gain at Sheffield Crown Court in January, 1974. The court was told that both men had luxury homes in Ecclesall and ran expensive cars, but the police raid had caused their business – part of which was legitimate – to collapse and they were left insolvent.

It was not only the twilight worlds of drugs, vice and porn which posed problems for the authorities. In 1968 Chief Constable Barker wrote: "The year has brought another disconcerting social trend to the area, that of open public disorder with hooliganism at and around football grounds."

A particularly nasty incident occurred in the 1971-72 season, following Derby County's 4-0 defeat of Sheffield United at Bramall Lane. A twenty three year old United supporter set about two men, whom he supposed to be Derby followers, with a four foot iron stake, fracturing the skull of one man and the jaw of the other. Both victims were Sheffield men. The attacker was imprisoned for five years. At Hillsborough in December, 1974 an invasion of the pitch at the Sheffield Wednesday v. Manchester United game was prevented only by a large force of police officers. At this match there were 106 arrests.

From the mid 1960s onwards violent crime progressively increased. Reported woundings rose from 163 in 1965 to 723 in 1972, and to 1,216 by 1980. A case which aroused much feeling occurred in 1971 when a sixty-three year old blind man was attacked in his home on the Manor estate. He was playing his violin when two men broke in and set about him with a wheelbrace. The attackers were arrested when police received information following a photograph of the victim's injuries in the local press. Sentencing each man to fifteen years imprisonment, Mr. Justice Caulfield told them: "I think the whole of society will condemn you."

By 1976 the situation had deteriorated still further and in his annual report, the Chief Constable, Stanley Barratt, wrote: "Of all the different categories of crime, violence still remains the most disturbing . . . . While it has become a cliche to say that we live in a violent society, the hard facts of the situation cannot be denied. People, especially young people, far too readily turn to the use of force to express their feelings or to relieve their frustrations. Weapons, especially knives, are far more frequently used than by the last generation which grew up in the aftermath of a violent war. The causes and answers to violence remain as elusive as ever."

Although violence was generally on a rapid upsurge, the final abolition of the death penalty in November, 1965 did not result in any immediate increase in cases of murder in Sheffield. In the ten years following – up to the end of 1974 – there were twenty-two cases[1], many of a domestic background.

None was more sensational in its circumstances than that of Mrs. Winifred Jessica Hepplewhite, whose weighted and trussed body was found floating in the River Tyne at Gateshead on March 10th, 1966. The dead woman, aged forty-nine, was identified by her husband, Kenneth Hepplewhite, a police sergeant at Woodseats. She had not been seen since the evening of January 31st, when she left the West End Hotel, Glossop Road, where she worked. An inquest found strangulation to be the cause of death, and the body was stated to have been in the water for a considerable time.

On March 22nd Kenneth Hepplewhite, aged thirty-five, was charged with the murder. He had been involved in a road accident near Wetherby in the late evening of January 31st, while driving his Hillman Husky

---

[1]One of these cases resulted in acquittal for the defendant, who was found to have acted in self-defence.

northwards. This was the last day on which his wife was see alive, and a police officer, called to the accident, remembered noticing a sack in the rear of Hepplewhite's car.

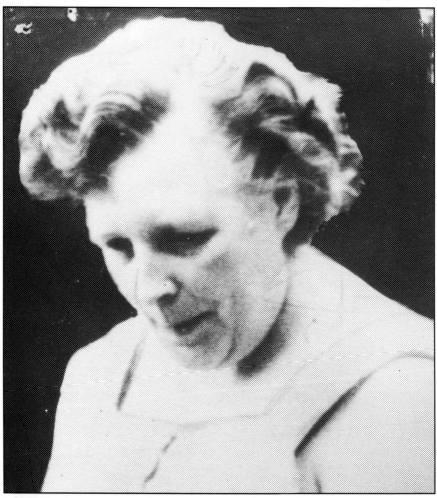

Winifred Jessica Hepplewhite, formerly of Fir Street, Sheffield. Her weighted and trussed body was found in the River Tyne at Gateshead on March 10th, 1966. Photo: Sheffield Newspapers Ltd.

Hepplewhite was tried at Leeds Assizes in June, 1966. Forty-nine witnesses were involved in the case and the court heard of a tempestuous relationship between the defendant and the deceased, who was said by witnesses to have become very aggressive and antagonistic towards her husband after being injured in a coach crash a year earlier. It was alleged that she had threatened to divorce him on the day of her disappearance. After deliberating for over three hours the jury found Hepplewhite guilty, recommending mercy, but the judge passed the only sentence possible on such a verdict – life imprisonment. Hepplewhite maintained his innocence throughout, saying that when his wife disappeared he simply thought that she had left him, as she had so often threatened to do. Detective Superintendent Ian Forbes, of Scotland Yard's Murder Squad, who arrested Hepplewhite, later described the case as one of the most gruesome of his career. He wrote in his autobiography, *Squadman*, "It was a story that might have been devised by that master of the macabre, Alfred Hitchcock."

The death of Albert Glendower Glossop led to a major murder hunt in the city in 1969. Glossop, a fifty-seven year old warehouseman, left the Penny Black pub in Pond Street at 10.30 p.m. on Monday, August 17th. About half an hour later he was seen in Shoreham Street, walking towards his home in Charlotte Road, where he lived with his widowed mother. Shortly after midnight he was found by a patrolling policeman in Charles Street, lying unconscious with severe head wounds. He died the following day.

How Albert Glossop came to retrace his steps has never been established. A murder squad of up to eighty officers worked solidly for forty-five days but the case was never solved. There were extensive enquiries among the city's homosexuals and also among bus crews and taxi drivers, who, it was thought, may have carried the deceased back to the city centre. At the inquest an open verdict was recorded on Albert Glossop who, it was stated, "met his death as a result of injuries he received when he fell to the ground after being assaulted by some person unknown."

Just as Albert Glossop died from a fractured skull after being assaulted, so did John Wortley six years later. Similarly, the person or persons responsible for Wortley's death have so far never been found. The only difference in the two unsolved mysteries is that, while the coroner's open verdict on Glossop resulted in his death being classed as unsolved manslaughter, the verdict that John Wortley was "murdered by person or persons unknown" meant that city police had the only undetected murder in living memory on their books.

John Wortley, a sixty-six year old car park attendant, was found battered to death next to his pay kiosk in the Arundel Gate multi-storey car park during the evening of June 5th, 1975. A small, frail man, weighing only seven stones, he had been struck with a fire extinguisher and robbed of the contents of the till – fifty-nine pounds. The irony was that he should not have been working on that day, but was standing in for someone else.

Initially the police had what seemed like some useful leads. A wages slip found close to the scene and items of blood-stained clothing spotted by dry

Top left:
Albert Glendower Glossop. Died after an assault in Charles Street, 1969.
Centre:
Terivia Matilda Cameron. Stangled at her home in Upperthorpe, 1982.
Bottom right:
John Wortley. Killed in Arundel Gate multi-storey car park, 1975.
Photos: Sheffield Newspapers Ltd.

cleaners raised hopes, as did an anonymous caller who telephoned murder squad detectives and claimed that two attackers were involved. A tape of his call was played on local radio but the caller was never identified. Eventually the trail went cold and after six weeks the large police investigation, which had involved at times 120 officers, was scaled down.

Over the years there have been numerous tip-offs and snippets of information which have spread the investigation as far as the Channel Islands. Some of those who contacted the police were doubtless motivated by the thousand pound reward offered by National Car Parks, others were attempts by members of the underworld to curry favour or settle old scores.

Detectives have never ruled out the possibility that John Wortley knew his attacker and that he was killed so that he could not talk after finding someone rifling the till. Several aspects of the inquiry were never cleared up: a man was seen in the kiosk, talking to John Wortley shortly before he was found dead – the man never came forward; a green Hillman Minx, though to have been about twenty years old at the time of the murder, was parked in the car park, but the driver has never been found; a man in his forties was seen changing a wheel on a car in the reserved section of the car park – a woman was with him but neither has ever been found; at about the time that John Wortley met his death a man in a pinstripe suit took a taxi from Fitzalan Square to Manchester – he did not book in at the hotel at which he alighted and was never traced.

It may be that one of these clues eventually leads to the killer. Certainly the police do not give up hope. In June, 1985, on the tenth anniversary of the murder, Detective Chief Superintendent Robin Herold, head of South Yorkshire C.I.D., told the *Star*: "Somebody, somewhere must have suspicions. Somebody has lived with this killing on their conscience for ten years. I believe one day we will catch him." In the meantime the longest murder investigation ever mounted in Sheffield continues.

A city house burglary in 1972, in which a safe – reported to contain £50,000 in cash and £10,000 worth of jewellery – was stolen, was described by the *Star* as "Sheffield's classic crime of the century."

On 10th March, 1972, burglars broke into a large, detached house on Sandygate Road, Crosspool. Unable to gain entry at the rear of the premises, they forced their way in through the front door and, while the occupant, a sixty-seven year old widow, slept, they removed the bulky safe, dragging it from the house wrapped in a Persian carpet. The widow, a retired market trader, was said by her daughter to have kept the money and valuables in the house because she did not like banks. None of the loot was ever recovered, nor was anyone convicted for the burglary.

Seven years after the Sandygate Road burglary a security guard, delivering wages to Stanley Tools Ltd on Rutland Road, was clubbed to the ground by two men and robbed of £71,000 in cash. The robbery occurred at

8.35 a.m. on October 31st, 1979, as a security van made a weekly delivery. The driver took a cash box from the van while the guard remained inside. As he entered the building he was attacked from behind. His goggles were smashed, ammonia was sprayed in his eyes, and his shoulder broken with an iron bar. His two assailants escaped in a waiting Triumph 1300. They were pursued by a Stanley employee, who gave chase in a works van but was quickly left behind. The escape car, stolen earlier in Leicester, was found in Brunswick Road. Despite descriptions being issued and a police reconstruction of the incident, neither cash nor robbers were ever seen again.

Serious crime in Sheffield during the 1970s was not solely concerned with spectacular thefts. A case heard at Sheffield Crown Court in March, 1973 was compared by the prosecution to Agatha Christie's *The case of the frightened witness*. On trial was thirty-two year old car dealer, described as "the central figure in a chronicle of intimidation and coercion". Mr. Donald Herrod Q.C. told the jury: "I am sure it will not have escaped your attention in looking at the demeanour of various people who came into the witness box that one after another of them was obviously frightened of giving evidence."

The defendant was said to have been known as 'The Debt Collector'. Among the charges on which he was convicted was one of blackmailing a city centre tailor. Another charge related to a firm of motor dealers who were told that their unwillingness to do business with the defendant would cost them "a fortune in tyres". Subsequently thirty-seven tyres on their vehicles were found to have been slashed. It was alleged that another car dealer who crossed 'The Debt Collector's' path had the windows of his bungalow smashed, and was told, "for a fiver the windows went in . . . . for a tenner the bungalow will go down."

The jury heard of a payment to a man in Leeds Prison, who was propositioned to make a statement that he had broken the tailor's window, and of the man's fear of violence at the hands of someone referred to as 'The Hammer Man'. It was also revealed that 'The Debt Collector' had previously been the principal prosecution witness in a case where a policeman was jailed for five years for corruption.

The prosecution alleged that people lived in fear of the defendant, who seemed to have the idea that he could ride roughshod over others and use strongarm methods to collect money, sometimes money which was legitimately owed to him. Defending, Mr. Harry Ognall said: "This is not a Mafia case, not a protection racket case", but, passing sentence, Judge Dean Q.C. told the defendant: "You put yourself above the law . . . . Your conduct is like a cancer in the body of society which, if allowed to spread, will destroy it." 'The Debt Collector' was imprisoned for eight years. Later the term was reduced to six years on appeal. Two detectives who led investigations into the case were praised by the judge for "clearing out a cesspit" and "making Sheffield a better and cleaner place."

The 1960s and 70s brought about some significant developments in the administration of criminal justice. Hard on the heels of the 'Rhino Whip' affair came the 1964 Police Act, which, as a direct result of the Sheffield scandal, imposed a statutory obligation on Chief Constables to investigate every complaint against the force. The same Act replaced the old Watch Committees with Police Authorities, comprising local councillors and magistrates in the ratio of two to one. The abolition of Quarter Sessions and Assizes made way for Sheffield Crown Court, established in 1972 and, six years later, the new Magistrates Courts were opened at a cost of three million pounds. Plans had been under way for a new court building in the city since 1936.

There were changes too in local police organisation. In 1967 the Sheffield force merged with that of Rotherham, and in 1974 local authority reorganisation included Barnsley and Doncaster in the new South Yorkshire Police.

The establishment of Regional Crime Squads throughout England and Wales heralded the beginnings of provincial forces' fight against serious crime, using permanent specialist squads. The Sheffield branch of the R.C.S. began with four seconded officers in 1964. After the Drug Squad in 1967 came other specialist units like the Commercial Branch – formed within the C.I.D. in 1970 to investigate company fraud, the Stolen Vehicle Squad and the Metal Squad. The latter, operating from Attercliffe police station, was formed to deal with the large amount of stolen high-value metal which was circulating in the city.

Police recruitment posed a major problem until economic recession began to affect general employment in the latter half of the 1970s. But despite low manpower, detection rates remained consistently higher than the national average. In 1965, with the Sheffield force almost one third under strength, 55.56 per cent of reported crimes were detected, compared to 39.2 per cent nationally. Ironically, the Sheffield detection rate fell to its lowest ever figure of 45.91 per cent in 1980, a year in which the force was at almost full numerical strength[2].

One reason for the fall, advanced by the Chief Constable, James Brownlow, was the national steelworkers' strike, which began on January 2nd, 1980 and continued for thirteen weeks. Large contingents of police officers were transferred from normal duties to the scenes of mass picketing, notably Hadfield's East Hecla Works in Vulcan Road.

On February 14th an estimated fifteen hundred demonstrators gathered in Vulcan Road with the intention of preventing the Hadfield's workforce from entering the premises. Seven other police forces assisted South Yorkshire and all but fifteen employees entered the works.

---

[2]The South Yorkshire force establishment in 1985 was 2,872 officers. Of these 1,066 were based in the three Sheffield divisions.

Commenting on the steel strike in his annual report, the Chief Constable praised his force and described as "commendable" the relationships the police had been able to maintain throughout the strike with local political leaders and trade union officials.

Twelve months to the day since the beginning of the steel strike, there occurred an incident which focussed even more media attention upon policing in Sheffield.

Late in the evening of Friday, January 2nd, 1981 two uniformed police officers, out on routine vice patrol, came upon a brown Rover 2000 car parked in Melbourne Avenue, Broomhill. In the car the officers, Sergeant Robert Ring and P.C. Robert Hydes, found a man and a local prostitute. The man told the officers that his name was Peter Williams but their suspicions were aroused when a radio check to the police computer revealed a discrepancy between the registration plates and the description of the car. Both occupants were taken to Hammerton Road police station, where the man admitted that his real name was Peter William Sutcliffe. Later, when questioned in Dewsbury by West Yorkshire detectives, he also admitted that he was the man responsible for the Yorkshire Ripper murders.

Sutcliffe, who might well have claimed his first Sheffield victim that night, was later sentenced at the Old Bailey to life imprisonment for thirteen murders and seven attempted murders, all of women, stretching back five-and-a-half years. Sgt. Ring, aged forty-seven and with twenty-seven years police service, and P.C. Hydes, thirty-one and still a probationer, were catapulted to world-wide fame by newspaper, radio and television. They received the attention modestly, Sgt. Ring telling interviewers that the arrest was "just normal coppering". Both officers received commendations from the trial judge, from the Chief Constable, and from South Yorkshire Police Authority, who in a unique gesture awarded the officers £100 each for "exceptional diligence".

The arrest of Sutcliffe brought to an end a manhunt which had cost millions of pounds and had been a tremendous drain on police resources, especially those of the West Yorkshire force, in whose area many of the murders had taken place. Police and public breathed an enormous sigh of relief and praises and gratitude was heaped upon the South Yorkshire force in general and Sgt. Ring and P.C. Hydes in particular. It was South Yorkshire Police's finest hour.

RECENT EVENTS

Crime in Sheffield in the 1980s continued on its upward trend. During the first half of the decade indictable offences reported in the three city police divisions rose by an overall fifty-nine per cent to total 36,300 in 1984.

House burglaries in the city numbered 5,340, having trebled in ten years. In March, 1985 even the Chief Constable, Peter Wright, fell victim when his Dore home was entered while he and his wife watched television. The intruder, who had stolen a wallet from a bedroom, escaped after a struggle but was later arrested and imprisoned for two years.

The record haul for an armed robbery in Sheffield was set on February 7th, 1983, when two masked men held up a Post Office van in Midland

Scene of £83,873 Post Office van robbery, February 7th, 1983. Photo: Andrew C. Smith.

Street, Heeley, and stole £83,873 in cash. The van was engaged on cash deliveries to sub-post offices around the city and had just completed its first call, in Shoreham Street, when the raiders struck. After threatening the driver and his assistant with a shotgun, the men took control of the van, driving it a short distance and picking up a third man, before transferring the mail bags containing the cash to a Ford Granada.

Two men were later charged in connection with the robbery. The Post Office driver, who admitted passing information via a link-man to the robbers, was sentenced to five years imprisonment. He had altered his route on the day of the robbery, so that Shoreham Street was the first call instead of the last. The link-man, who pleaded not guilty, was convicted and sentenced to eight years. The men who carried out the robbery, one of whom was believed to be a Liverpudlian, have so far not been found and the record amount of cash stolen remains unrecovered.

Sub-post offices have, in recent years, become increasingly the targets of armed robbers. In October, 1984 staff and an elderly customer were threatened at knife-point when three men stole £29,058 at Verdon Street sub-post office, Burgreave. In the following months sub-post offices at Foxhill, Norfolk Park, Ecclesall and Glossop Road were attacked with varying degrees of success. In all instances firearms were brandished by the raiders.

On September 21st, 1984 city detectives were faced with two armed robbery inquiries on the same day. In the morning two security guards were held up outside the Midland Bank in Albert Terrace Road, Upperthorpe and were relieved of £12,000 by two men, one wielding a shotgun. In the afternoon a man wearing a crash helmet and pointing what appeared to be an automatic pistol ordered a cashier at the National and Provincial Building Society in Norfolk Street to fill a carrier bag with the contents of her till.

April 4th, 1985 brought another major security van robbery. Six men ambushed a Securicor van on Vulcan Road, Tinsley and, after grabbing the driver and pointing a pistol at a guard, they made off with £74,000. Rewards of £5,000 by Securicor and £7,000 by an insurance company were offered but neither cash nor robbers have so far come to light.

The homicide rate fluctuated sharply during the decade. In 1983 there were fourteen killings in the city, a figure which was double the previous highest of seven recorded in 1975 and again in 1982. Unlike other criminal statistics, homicide rates tend not to be influenced by the wider social factors. Cases are frequently unique in their circumstances and the totals of homicides for each decade prior to the present one show an increase disproportionately lower than for other types of offence.

The most gruesome of the 1983 killings were those of three members of the Laitner family, stabbed to death on October 23rd in their Dore home, only hours after celebrating a family wedding. The killer, Arthur Hutchinson, was captured by police in his native North East two weeks later, after one of the biggest manhunts ever seen in Britain. Forty-three year old Hutchinson, a man with a criminal record going back to the age of twelve, was already on the run when he killed the Laitners. He had escaped from police custody in Selby. On September 14th, 1984 he was sentenced to life imprisonment with a recommendation that he serve at least eighteen years.

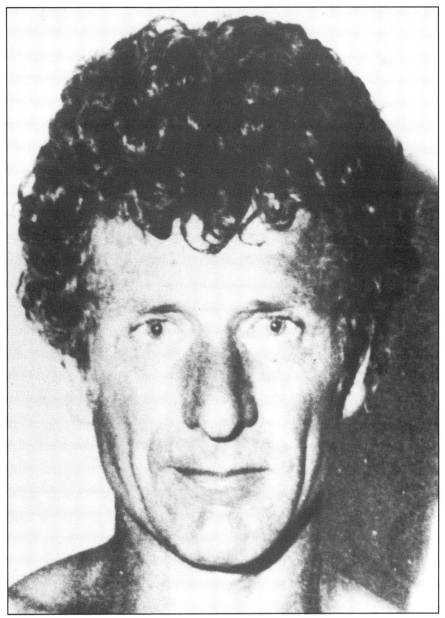

Arthur Hutchinson. Sentenced to life imprisonment in 1984 for the murder of three members of the Laitner family.
Photo: Sheffield Newspapers Ltd.

Two other local murders have frustrated police. On July 8th, 1982 the body of Jamaican born Terivia Matilda Cameron, a fifty-nine year old retired nurse, was dragged by neighbours from her blazing flat in Addy Close, Upperthorpe. Mrs. Cameron, who was partly paralysed, was known to smoke in bed and initially this was thought to be the cause of the fire and her death. However, when a post-mortem revealed death had been caused by strangulation, a murder inquiry was launched with one hundred and twenty five police officers. The motive for the killing appeared to be robbery and it was believed that whoever strangled the woman had set fire to the flat in an attempt to cover their tracks. To date the person or persons have never been caught and, as with the case of John Wortley, the police files remain open.

Eight months after Terivia Cameron's death, another middle-aged woman who lived alone was found dead in similar circumstances. Patricia Hurst, aged fifty-six, was battered to death in her home in Ecclesall Road on March 10th, 1983. Her home was also set alight and the motive seemed again to be robbery. A twenty-five year old woman, who owned a nearby poodle parlour, and her seventeen year old boyfriend were later charged with murder. After two trials both were acquitted, the woman being sentenced to three years for arson and the youth a similar sentence after admitting robbery. The Director of Public Prosecutions later confirmed that the file in this case was closed.

The drug problem which began in the 1960s shows no sign of relenting. In 1984, 318 people were charged with 751 drug related offences in South Yorkshire. Of these, 199 offences concerned Class A drugs (opiates etc) and 443 Class B (e.g. amphetamines). The police achieved some notable results in Sheffield, particularly in their battle against suppliers. In 1982 a local junkie-cum-dealer, who was said to have made £3,000 a week over a long period out of selling drugs in city centre pubs, was imprisoned for eight years. A detective sergeant, convicted of conspiring with the dealer to supply drugs, was jailed for three years. The following year a research chemist who set up an amphetamine factory at Sheffield University was imprisoned for three years and fined £4,000.

In one of several large seizures of heroin, a Sheffield man was found in possession of two and a half kilos in 1982, on arrival in England from Pakistan. The following year four Pakistani nationals, resident in Sheffield, were arrested and heroin with a street value of £170,000, plus £60,000 in cash, was recovered. In 1984 a Firth Park man was imprisoned for seven years for being in possession of heroin worth £100,000. It had been smuggled into Britain by a courier, concealed among vegetables. But these men were small-time compared with a Sheffield man charged in the south of England in mid 1985 with smuggling heroin worth two-and-a-half million pounds into the country from Pakistan. With such potential consignments threatening to hit the streets of South Yorkshire, it was no surprise when in late 1985 plans were announced to increase the county Drug Squad by almost a third to twenty-five officers.

Prostitution in Sheffield hit the national headlines in 1983 when, in October, city magistrates announced a policy of imposing the maximum £200 fine on persistent offenders who appeared before them. This coincided with efforts by the police to rid the Broomhall streets of the activities of prostitutes and their kerb-crawling clients. There were 514 prosecutions for soliciting in the city during the year, compared with 136 in 1982. In one case, shortly after the new policy was introduced, the Stipendary Magistrate, Ian Crompton, fined five women a total of £1,350 and told them: "I'm going to take the profit out of prostitution." Two weeks later a Hyde Park woman, who told the court she made no money out of prostitution, was fined £800 on four charges. Another, who said: "Every time I go out I get picked up by the police" was fined £400. In April, 1984, six months after the policy began, the magistrates reviewed the situation and softened their fines. In 1984 one hundred and seventy six women were prosecuted in the city for soliciting.

The most significant factor to affect local policing in the 1980s was undoubtedly the miners' strike, which began in March, 1984 and continued for twelve months. In his annual report, Chief Constable Peter Wright wrote of the strike: "Its impact on policing during 1984 has been profound, both directly in the demand mass picketing and its associated disorder has placed on police resources and also indirectly in its consequence in all other aspects of policing."
The first major incident in Sheffield relating to the strike occurred on April 19th. An estimated 7,000 people attended a Delegates' Conference of the National Union of Mineworkers at the City Hall and afterwards there were some disorderly scenes outside the hall. On the same day sixty-nine arrests were made after police drew truncheons at an incident outside the Sheffield Trades and Labour Club in Duke Street.
Orgreave Coking Plant was the location of the worst confrontations between police and miners, as pickets attempted to prevent lorries carrying coke from the plant to Scunthorpe steel works. On June 18th an estimated ten thousand pickets were met by police from forces all over England and Wales. Riot gear and a cavalry charge was the order of the day and ninety-three arrests were made.
The prosecution of many of the pickets arrested at Orgreave became a controversy in itself. After one forty-eight day trial at Sheffield Crown Court, fifteen men charged with riot were found not guilty and subsequently the Chief Constable halted proceedings against two hundred and twenty men who were alleged to have participated in some of the most

violent scenes in the dispute. The end result of prosecution cases in all South Yorkshire was that sixty-seven men were bound over to keep the peace.

Over three hundred South Yorkshire police officers were injured as a result of picket line disturbances, four of them seriously. The cost in financial terms of policing the dispute in the county was £18,898,000. The county force had to find a million pounds of this amount out of its annual budget, a situation which led to cuts in various areas, including training, repairs to buildings and the replacement of vehicles.

The most important effect, however, was the increase in crime, in Sheffield and in the county as a whole, during 1984. While police officers were deployed on strike duties, more criminals were escaping with the loot than ever before. Statistics for the year show the value of property stolen in the county to have risen from £12.68 million in 1983 to £20.03 million. The number of reported crimes in the county increased by 15 per cent, while the detection rate fell by 8.42 per cent to 40.71. In Sheffield 36,300 offences were reported – an increase of 1,653 on the previous year while the detection rate dropped to an all-time low of 43.22 per cent.

The Sheffield Metals Case, which began with a reported theft of ferro-alloys, used in the manufacture of stainless steel, and culminated in a series of trials during 1984-85, has been described as the biggest and most complex inquiry ever undertaken by South Yorkshire Police.

At the core of the case was a massive fraud on Napier Steels, an Oughtibridge subsidiary of Sheffield Twist Drill, who lost more than £1.7 million, but as the inquiry developed other offences of theft, burglary, arson, conspiracy, corruption and serious violence emerged. In all, forty seven arrests were made and eighteen people were prosecuted.

A sixty-four year old managing director was jailed for seven and a half years on twenty-five charges of corruption, a detective sergeant received a five year sentence, and a man who was described in one trial as a gangster and "one of the blackest villains in South Yorkshire" was given four-and-a-half years on charges which included conspiracy to commit arson at a private school. In a separate, but linked, case three Sheffield men received a total of twenty-one years for their involvement in the shooting of a scrap metal dealer as he drove along Sheffield Parkway in January, 1983.

The Metals Case came about through a liaison between sophisticated 'white-collar' criminals and ruthless underworld characters, linked by the common motivation of greed. Painstaking investigations went on for many months and certain aspects of the case revealed all too clearly the dangers faced by detectives in dealing with experienced and manipulative criminals.

After hearing of vendettas and violence, of offences covered up and criminals allegedly 'fitted up', Mr. Justice Glidewell told the jury in one of the principal trials in January, 1985: "You must have wondered whether you were hearing about Sheffield or Sicily at times during this trial." Certainly, with its ramifications and undertones of organised crime, there had been nothing comparable to the Metals Case in the long history of crime in Sheffield.

BIBLIOGRAPHY

Bailey V. (ed.) *Policing and punishment in 19th century Britain.* Croom Helm, 1981.

Bean J.P. *The Sheffield gang wars.* D. & D. Publications, 1981.

Bellamy J. *Crime and public order in the later middle ages.* R. & K.P., 1973.

Browning A. (ed.) *Memoirs of Sir John Reresby.* Jackson, 1936.

Castle J. *The pocket watch murderer.* Unpublished m/s in Sheffield City Libraries Local History Section.

Chesney K. *The Victorian underworld.* Temple Smith, 1970.

Chief Constable's Annual Reports 1935-84.

Cockburn J. S. *Crime in England 1550-1800.* Methuen, 1977.

Cox B., Shirley J., Short M. *The fall of Scotland Yard.* Penguin, 1977.

Criminal Chronology of York Castle. 1867.

Dewar D. *Hallamshire – A note on its Justices' Courts, Justices and Clerks,* 1975.

Forbes I. *'Squadman'.* W. H. Allen, 1973.

Hall T. W. (ed.) *Transcriptions of Sheffield Manorial Court Rolls.* J. W. Northend, 1926.

Hawson H. K. *The growth of a city 1893-1926.* J. W. Northend, 1968.

Holberry Society Bulletins. 1978 onwards.

Holberry Society Pamphlet. *Samuel Holberry – Sheffield's Revolutionary Democrat, 1978.*

Holland Dr. G. C. *The vital statistics of Sheffield.* 1843.

Judges A. V. (ed.) *The Elizabethan underworld.* R. & K.P., 1930.

Leader J. D. *Records of the burgery of Sheffield.* Sheffield Independent Press, 1897.

Leader R. E. *Sheffield in the 18th Century.* Sheffield Independent Press, 1901.

Leader R. E. *Reminiscences of Old Sheffield.* Leader and Sons, 1875.

Lister J. (ed.) *West Riding sessions record 1611-42.* Yorkshire Archeological Society, 1915.

McCall A. *The medieval underworld.* H. Hamilton, 1979.

McFarlane A. *The justice and the mare's ale.* Blackwell, 1981.

Mantoux P. *The industrial revolution in the 18th Century.* Methuen, 1961.

Mark Sir R. *In the office of constable.* Allen & Uwin, 1977.

Pearson G. *Hooligan – a study of respectable fears.* Macmillan, 1983.

Pollard S. *A history of labour in Sheffield.* Liverpool University Press, 1959.

Pollard S. *The ethics of the Sheffield outrages.* Transactions of the Hunter Archeological Society, Vol. 7.

Raine J. (ed.) *Depositions from the Castle of York relating to offences committed in the Northern Counties.* Surtees Society, Vol. 40, 1860.

Sheffield Local Register. Published by R. E. Leader until 1908.

Sheffield Red Book/Year Book, 1863-1975.

Sheffield Police Appeal Inquiry. HMSO, 1963.

Shore W. T. (ed.) *The trials of Charles Peace.* Hodge, 1926.

Sillitoe Sir P. *Cloak without dagger.* Cassell, 1955.

Sweeney C. *Transported in place of death.* Macmillan, 1981.

Tobias J. J. *Crime and industrial society in the 19th Century.* Batsford, 1967.
Walton M. *Sheffield – its story and its achievements.* SR Publishing, 1948.
Ward D. *King of the Lags.* Elek, 1962.
Winder T. (ed.) *An old Ecclesfield diary 1775-1845.* 1921.

INDEX